I0005284

Strategically Focused and Tactically Agile CIO

A Practitioner's Handbook
for Current and Future
Chief Information Officers

Michael Hugos

Center for Systems Innovation [c4si]
Chicago, Illinois USA

Copyright © 2013, Michael Hugos
www.MichaelHugos.com

Cover Picture Credit:
"Art from Code", Keith Peters, 2008
www.artfromcode.com

Table of Contents

1. Strategically Focused.................................1

   Relationship of IT Strategy to Organizational Strategy 2

   A Framework for Clear Thinking 7

   Move from Strategic Planning to Strategic Agility 10

   Strategic Guidelines for Designing IT Systems.............13

2. Tactically Agile.................................19

   Agility is a Process 20

   Loop 1: Monitoring and Deciding 24

   Loop 2: Improving Existing Processes 29

   Loop 3: Creating New Processes.................32

   Dynamics of the Agile IT Organization.........35

3. Core Techniques for Agility.....................39

   Just a Handful of Techniques.......................39

   Tactical Principles for Running Projects.........51

   Agile Project Management.............................55

   Five Questions Everyone Needs to Answer
   Every Day...59

4. The Agile 30-Day Blitz...........................65

   Benefits of Define – Design – Build Cycle.....................66

   Define – The Framework for Action 69

   Design – Workflow and Technical System.....................79

   Build – Systems Construction and Roll Out 87

5. Encounter with Complexity............................95

Case Studies: Two Wins, a Lose and a Draw.................96

Executive Checklist for Monitoring Development
Projects 103

About the Author...109

Chapter 1.

Strategically Focused

This handbook is dedicated to the idea that there is a set of highly effective strategies and tactics that chief information officers (CIOs) can apply to significantly increase the competitiveness and profitability of their companies. Even though information technology itself is changing rapidly, these strategies and tactics transcend any particular technology, and they remain relevant over time. I have applied them in a wide variety of businesses and fine tuned them for more than fifteen years. They deliver results that are consistently competent and occasionally brilliant.

They enable me to respond smartly to a wide variety of situations. Using them got me promoted from developer to manager to director and finally to CIO. As a CIO they helped me earn a seat at the boardroom table with other "C" level executives and my work was recognized with awards from three prominent IT industry magazines (CIO magazine, Computerworld and InformationWeek).

My purpose here is to describe a set of practical and pragmatic strategies and tactics to achieve and maintain focus and agility in your own performance and in that of your IT organization. In the high change, high risk, and highly competitive real-time economy that companies compete in today, CIOs make their most valuable contributions by continually evolving and enhancing the information technology (IT) infrastructure of their company so that it stays aligned with business strategy. This is where CIOs need to devote the bulk of their attention and their time. Although the CIO still remains responsible for the reliable day-to-day functioning of the IT infrastructure, that responsibility is not a CIO level job any more.

The CIO's most valuable contribution to business lies in the skill and imagination with which the technology is used to advance the strategic agenda of their company. It's not so much about squeezing more efficiency from internal IT operations; it's much more about how well you use technology to enable your company to respond to new opportunities to roll out new products and earn more revenue. Running an efficient and cost-effective IT organization has fallen off the list of the CIO's high value strategic capabilities because so many companies have learned these basic disciplines and company executives simply expect that kind of baseline performance now.

Once you align yourself with the value proposition that your company delivers to its customers then you open up a whole new world for yourself and for IT in your company. Driving company strategy and enabling the business to accomplish its goals is where the CIO adds the most value. With the rates of change in most companies, alignment work has become a full-time job in a way that was not the case even a few years ago. Today companies live in a world where advantage goes to the most agile and responsive companies, not just the most efficient ones.

Relationship of IT Strategy to Organizational Strategy

Just as the chief financial officer (CFO) is the senior person responsible for devising the capital structure best suited to a company's business needs, the CIO is the senior person responsible for making sure that the company's IT infrastructure best supports its business needs. The CIO is the senior level liaison between the business and technical sides of an organization. The CIO is the person who helps define and translate business goals and strategies into systems performance requirements

2

and oversees a portfolio of IT development projects to deliver systems that meet these requirements.

In the information age, the competent and dynamic use of information technology is a requirement that all organizations must meet in order to succeed. IT underpins every operation within an organization, and in fact it is hard to speak of operations and IT as separate entities any more. They are so intertwined and most business operations are so utterly dependent on information technology that it is usually pointless to think of them separately.

Therefore any valid business strategy rests on assumptions that the organization already has or can soon acquire the information systems it needs to achieve performance levels called for by the strategy. Strategies calling for operating capabilities and performance levels that cannot be attained are strategies doomed to fail. Perhaps 20 years ago IT considerations were of secondary concern to business strategists. Now IT considerations are central to any viable business strategy, but they require a commonly used framework for clear thinking and communication.

Business Strategy sets IT Strategy

All businesses have a set of goals either explicitly stated in a formal business plan or implicitly stated in the culture and conversations within the senior management team. As the CIO you need to know these business goals. Make sure you know them by heart.

Once you discover the organization's goals, the next step is to define a strategy or strategies to accomplish these goals. Remember, a strategy is simply a way of using the means or capabilities available to a business to achieve its goals. Often, a business executes its strategy by building or enhancing systems to do the things called for by the strategy.

Good strategy starts with asking the right questions. Strategy is the result you get from answering the questions you ask. Strategy that comes from answers to the wrong questions is useless strategy even if the answers themselves are correct. This is what is meant when people say generals often have great strategies to fight the last war (instead of strategies to fight the war they are in).

Generals, and all the rest of us, have a tendency to ask questions that are no longer all that relevant. We ask questions pertaining to the details of a situation that is now passed. We tend to ask these questions because we already know the answers. We learned them from our past experience. The trick is to learn from our experience and yet remember that the future will be different in some important respects from our experience in the past.

Here are some questions to ponder as you think about your IT strategy: What can IT do to enable my organization to accomplish its goals?; What business initiatives are planned over what time period?; What operating capabilities does the organization need to successfully carry out these initiatives?; What is the conceptual design of the IT systems infrastructure that will enable the company to posses the operating capabilities it needs?; How can the existing IT infrastructure best be leveraged to meet company needs?

Defining IT Strategy

To define your IT strategy, begin by listing a set of desired performance criteria that IT should meet in order to enable the business to accomplish its goals. Robert Kaplan and David Norton in their landmark 1992 Harvard Business Review article, "The Balanced Scorecard – Measures That Drive Performance" defined four perspectives that create a comprehensive view of an organization's performance.

Define the desired performance criteria that you expect IT to meet from these four different perspectives: 1) *Financial Perspective* – the financial performance measures you want IT to achieve; 2) *Customer Perspective* – things that external and internal customers want from IT; 3) *Business Perspective* – the business processes IT must excel at to accomplish company goals; and 4) *Learning Perspective* – how the IT organization will continue to learn and improve its ability to accomplish company goals

Brainstorm a large list of criteria under each of the four perspectives. Then review the lists and select four to eight of the most important performance criteria. If you can position IT to deliver the capabilities that meet these criteria, then the IT organization has accomplished its mission.

For instance, you may define financial criteria such as build new systems for X dollars and be able to operate them for Y dollars per year. Customer measures could track activities that provide customers with capabilities to do a range of activities such as look up products, enter orders, pay bills and interact with customer service. Business criteria track things such as: how well your systems handle a certain level of transactions per minute; how well they scale up to manage additional transaction volumes, and how quickly they can be learned by new users who need them to do their jobs. Learning measures demonstrate how well your system provides users with the data and reports they need to assess and improve their performance on an on-going basis.

Next, decide to achieve these criteria in dramatically new ways. Ask the question, "What seems currently impossible, but if it could be done, would dramatically change the way we do business?" Look for ways to use systems to change the business landscape, to give your organization a significant competitive advantage by doing something new and different.

Systems can be used to open up opportunities to either increase revenue or decrease costs. Systems can increase revenue by: creating new distribution channels; erecting barriers to entry by competitors; reducing customers' ability to substitute another product for your product; and helping the company anticipate and respond quickly to market demands. Systems can decrease costs by: improving product quality; increasing production rates; decreasing production and operating costs.

The ways in which systems accomplish these opportunities will either create structural change in the way an industry operates, or it will support and enhance traditional industry products and procedures. Great competitive advantages can be gained if ways are found to create structural change in an industry. This is what changes the business landscape. It is said that all you need to do is to be 10% new in any field to start a fortune, and companies that create structural change become leaders in their industries.

Remember, a system is always people, process, and technology – not just technology. Define and design the process first, and then put the people and technology into place to support it. At the same time, keep in mind the capabilities of the people and technology available, and design a process that is realistic given those capabilities. In other words, adjust your ends to your means. Good strategy starts with a clear understanding of what is possible.

One last point to remember about strategic IT projects is this. The executive sponsors on the business side need to remain actively involved with the project in an oversight and advisory role throughout the project's life cycle. If no senior managers take an interest in this role then either the goals that the IT strategy addresses are not really that important to the business, or people believe the strategy is flawed and doubt that the goals can be accomplished. In either case, you as the CIO should be aware of this. If that is the case, change your goals or your strategy if you want to remain part of senior management in your organization.

A Framework for Clear Thinking

Before we go further, let's define our terms. What exactly do we mean when we say strategy – especially in the context of the CIO's two main responsibilities? Strategy, tactics, goals, objectives, missions, and milestones – we often toss these words about in various vague, undisciplined, and confusing combinations. Most of the time terms such as goals and objectives or strategies and tactics are used interchangeably. The precise meaning of the words gets lost and so the clarity of thinking that these words can support is also lost.

If we hope to gain any real value from these words then we owe it to ourselves to be very precise and clear in the way we use them with both our executive peers and our staff members. Otherwise, they become trite phrases, macho imagery, or smokescreens for incompetence. The CIO needs to apply these terms in an IT context so as to identify appropriate strategic operating capabilities and performance levels for the rest of the organization. Exhibit 1.1 illustrates how these terms relate to each other.

Exhibit 1.1 Framework for Clear Thinking

Applied Strategy & Tactics

The vision of what the business wants to become is articulated by a set of goals.

Business Vision

The goals and the strategies to accomplish them are designed to make maximum use of the company's capabilities.

GOAL 1   **GOAL 2**   **GOAL 3**

Objective A   **Objective B**   **Objective C**

The strategy devised to accomplish a goal defines the objectives that are necessary and sufficient to do so.

Project Plan & Budget

		Cost
Objective A		
Task 1		
Task 2		
Task 3		$999
Objective B		
Task 4		
Task 5		$99
Objective C		
Task 6		$999
Task 7		
...		$9,999

Tactics are used to achieve objectives. Tactics are the methods you use to get things done. The sequence of tasks shown on the project plan reflects the tactics and techniques being used.

Business Vision - This is a statement of the company's purpose, why it exists, what it aspires to. The business vision of the company is articulated by a set of goals that define what the company will strive for and where the company will invest its resources.

Goal (or Mission) - A goal is a qualitative statement that describes a state of affairs or an accomplishment necessary for the business to become what it wants to become (the business vision). An example of a goal is, "Strengthen and grow the national accounts sales program." Another example would be, "Develop an e-business infrastructure to take advantage of market trends."

Strategy - Strategy can be defined as simply, "the deliberate application of means to achieve business vision and goal-related ends". Strategy is the art of using the means - business capabilities - available to a company to achieve its ends – its business goals. The degree to which a strategy is effective depends on a clear understanding of what is possible. The purpose of strategy is to maximize possibilities for the successful application of all means available. Strategies are used to coordinate the accomplishment of goals or missions.

Objective (or Milestone) - Unlike the business vision or a goal, an objective must be quantitative - a statement that defines a specific, measurable achievement necessary to accomplish a goal. The strategy that a business uses to accomplish a goal defines the objectives that must be achieved along the way. Objectives are the specific, measurable milestones that must be reached to accomplish a goal or mission. The key characteristic of an objective is that progress and final achievement can be clearly reported with standardized units of measure. An example of an objective is, "Increase sales in the healthcare sector this year by 15%."

Plan - A plan is a non-repetitive set of tasks that leads to the achievement of a new objective. A plan is not to be confused with an operating schedule, which is a repetitive set of tasks that are used to perpetuate an already existing state of affairs. The situation, the objectives defined and the tactics being applied guide the creation of a plan. The sequence of tasks shown on the project plan reflects the tactics and techniques that are being used. (See Exhibit 1.1.)

Tactics - Tactics are the execution and control of actions needed to carry out the business strategies and achieve objectives. Tactics effectively coordinate people, processes, and technology to achieve objectives that are defined by the business strategy. Tactics are the methods used to get things done.

Techniques - A technique is a well-defined action or behavior producing a pre-defined result. A technique is a systematic procedure by which a task is accomplished. Combining techniques into useful sequences creates tactics.

Move from Strategic Planning to Strategic Agility

Formulating IT strategy in the high change, high-risk environments we live in today is an iterative process of definition and redefinition. Our companies may go through formal strategic planning cycles every three or four years but every year in between and every quarter of each year CIOs must update and adjust their IT strategies to best respond to the way their world evolves. Gone are the days when IT strategies could be rigid, multi-year plans that laid out each activity in detail and then simply required people to do as they were told. People may actually be able to do the things they are told but with rigid plans they inevitably find themselves performing tasks that no longer relate to the real world and the real needs of their organization.

The point to understand is that a company's goals remain reasonably steady over a two to four year period but the IT strategies employed to accomplish those business goals may need to be changed every year or even more frequently. Like setting a ship's course, a strategy is a way of steering toward a goal – of getting from here to there. The real world unfolds in unexpected ways that may push you off your expected course so you make mid-course corrections (strategy corrections) as needed. But you are not just flailing about because you are always steering the IT organization toward a steady destination (the business goals).

Therefore, the IT strategy formulation process has a sequence of four steps to guide people through the cycle (see Exhibit 1.2). These steps are: 1) Map out the big picture; 2) Decide how to get from here to there; 3) Act effectively to manage risk; and 4) Evaluate changes

Exhibit 1.2. Four Steps to Strategy Formulation

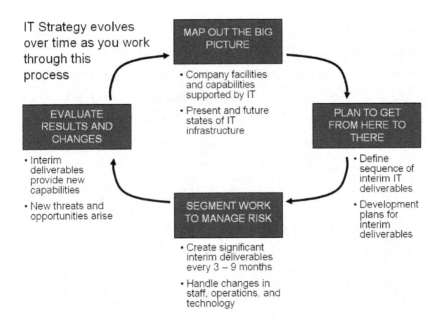

Map out the big picture means literally drawing a map that shows the territory in which your company operates. Use the map to identify the facility locations of your company at present and the locations that your company wants to open in the future. Usually the maps you draw will be more than just geographical maps. You also need to draw maps of the markets your company serves, maps that compare your systems capabilities to your competitors' capabilities, and maps that describe and compare the IT infrastructure of your company and its competitors. These maps, charts, diagrams, and lists define and identify where your company is at present and where it wants to be in the future. This future destination is the destination that all your IT strategies aim to reach. There can be no coherent strategy until people understand where they are trying to go.

Decide how to get from here to there means just that. When you understand where you are at present and where you want to go then you can make calculations about how far you have to go. You can also define some milestones or interim destinations along the way.

The last several decades of experience in the IT profession teaches us not to attempt "big bang" strategies. These types of strategies try to move IT organizations directly from where they are to where they want to be in one mighty leap and they usually fail. Instead define a sequence of interim destinations that create a path to follow to get you to the desired final destination. Then make your calculations for getting from where you are currently to the next interim destination on your path.

Act effectively to manage risk requires that you make sure the journey between these interim destinations can be accomplished in three to nine month steps that each produce value in their own right. The interim destination you reach in three to nine months cannot be just some midway point that still requires more work in order to be of any tangible value. In the context of IT this means that the interim destination must be a functioning system or operating process not just an analysis document or a set of specifications. The system must be able to go into production and begin repaying some of the cost of the work to produce it.

Design each three to nine month step so that changes in staffing, operations, and technology are affordable and manageable. Remember that systems are people, procedures, and technology combined in a coordinated way. Do not attempt changes in these three areas that are beyond the capability and capacity of your organization. Be honest about what is possible and what is probable.

Evaluate changes happens upon completion of each three to nine month step. The interim destination you reach at the end of each step provides a base from which to take the next step but does not lock the IT organization into any rigid, preset sequence of next steps. The world will probably have changed in some way in the last three to nine months. Now is your opportunity to pause for a moment to check out the lay of the land again.

Reaching an interim destination gives you a position and new capabilities you did not possess before. How can you best use this position and your new capabilities to capitalize on the opportunities that change may have brought your way? Or you can consider how best to counter a threat that just emerged. Either way, you make your decisions in light of the need to continue steering the IT organization toward providing the capabilities needed by the company to reach its stated goals.

Strategic Guidelines for Designing IT Systems

System designs reflect IT strategies and enable the company to achieve its performance targets. Good strategies and good system designs are two sides of the same coin. All system designs are not created equal. Some designs and the strategies they support are clearly superior to others, and there is an objective way to identify these superior designs.

Shown below are five positive guidelines and two negative guidelines for designing systems that reflect IT strategies (they are summarized in Exhibit 1.3). The best system designs follow all seven of these guidelines. A passable design can ignore one of them as long as it isn't the first guideline. However, any design that disregards more than two of these guidelines is fatally flawed and will lead to failure.

Positive Guidelines

Closely align systems projects with business goals - For any systems development project to be a success it must directly support the company to achieve one or more of its goals. No new system can be effective until you have first identified or created the business opportunity that will make the system worth building and no new system will bring any sustained benefit to your company unless it supports the efficient exploitation of the business opportunity it was built to address.

Use systems to change the competitive landscape - Look for tasks and activities that seem impossible today, but if they could be done, would fundamentally and positively change the ways your company does business. Put yourself in your customers' shoes. In the words of the Nordstrom's motto, think of what would "surprise and delight" your customers. Look for opportunities to create a transformation or value shift in your market. Find ways to do things that provide dramatic cost savings or productivity increases. Place yourself in your competitor's shoes and think of what course you could take that would be the least likely to be foreseen or quickly countered or copied. As long as you are able to do something of value that your competitors cannot, you have an advantage.

Leverage the strengths of existing systems - System design embodies strategy. When existing systems have proven to be stable and responsive over time, find ways to incorporate them into the design of new systems. The purpose of strategy is to use the means available to the organization to best accomplish its goal. Build new systems on the strengths of older systems. Nature uses the same principle in the evolutionary process. New systems provide value only in so far as they provide new business capabilities. Time spent replacing old systems with new systems that do essentially the same things will not, as a general rule, provide enough value to justify the cost.

Use the simplest combination of technology and business procedures to achieve as many different objectives as possible - A simple mix of technology and process that can achieve several different objectives increases the probability that these objectives can actually be achieved. This simple mix reduces the complexity and the risk associated with the work and spreads the cost across multiple objectives. Using a different technology or process to achieve each different project objective multiplies the cost and the complexity and reduces the overall probability of project success.

Structure the design so as to provide flexibility in the development sequence used to create the system - Break the system design into separate components or objectives, and whenever possible, run the work on individual objectives in parallel. Try to prevent the achievement of one objective from becoming dependant on the achievement of another objective. In this way, delays in the work toward one objective will not impact the progress toward other objectives. Use people on the project who have skills that can be used to achieve a variety of different objectives. If you use the same technology to achieve several different objectives, it is much easier to shift people from one objective to another as needed because they use the same skill sets. Your project plan should foresee and provide for an alternative plan in case of failure or delays in achieving objectives as scheduled. The design of the system you build should allow you to cut some system features if needed and still be able to deliver solid value to the business.

Negative Guidelines

Do not try to build a system with a level of complexity that exceeds the organization's capabilities - The beginning of wisdom is a sense of what is possible. When defining business goals and the systems needed to reach those goals, aim for things that are within your reach. Set challenging goals but not hopeless goals. The people in your organization need to have confidence in themselves in order to rise to a challenge. Avoid exhausting their confidence in vain efforts to reach unrealistic goals.

Do not renew a project using the same people or the same system design after it has once failed - Redoubled hard work and effort are an inadequate response for ensuring the success of a project after it has once failed. People are probably demoralized after the first failure and will not rise to the challenge of doing the work again unless there are meaningful changes in the project approach. The new approach must clearly reflect what was learned from the previous failure and offer a better way to achieve the project objectives. ∞

Exhibit 1.3 Strategic Guidelines for Designing Systems

Strategic Guidelines for Designing Systems

POSITIVE

1. Closely align systems development projects with business goals and specific performance targets.

2. Use systems to change the business landscape.

3. Leverage the strengths of existing systems.

4. Use the simplest possible combination of technology and process to achieve the maximum number of objectives.

5. Structure the design so as to provide flexibility in the development sequence used to create the system.

NEGATIVE

6. Do not try to build a system whose complexity exceeds the organization's abilities to support it.

7. Do not renew a project using the same organization or the same system design after it has once failed.

Notes and Ideas for Action:

Notes and Ideas for Action:

Chapter 2.

Tactically Agile

Companies need to be agile to keep up with their markets, and IT organizations must be agile to stay aligned with their companies. As company strategy evolves over time, the CIO must constantly assess strategic changes and their impact on the IT organization. Does the existing infrastructure support the new business strategies? What new capabilities are needed? How can existing systems best be leveraged, and what new systems are needed?

Let's start by defining a tactically agile IT organization as one that senses and responds to environmental change efficiently and effectively. The two operative concepts here are "senses and responds"; and "efficiently and effectively". In other words, IT organizations must (1) constantly collect and analyze information to detect change; and (2) respond appropriately when changes are detected.

Agility is an on-going process, not just an occasional event. An agile IT organization is not an athlete one day and then a couch potato the next day. An IT organization cannot be agile unless all its members are agile, so agile work principles need to be understood and practiced by everyone. The diagram in Exhibit 2.1 outlines the process flow that creates agility throughout the IT organization. Note that agility is composed of three sub-processes or feedback loops that all run concurrently.

Agility is a Process

A simple model of the system dynamics used by such an organization is shown below. Agile operating principles and agile IT can be employed to drive three simultaneous feedback loops that make real-time operations possible. The first feedback loop provides awareness of a changing environment and identifies threats and opportunities (the Yin-Yang symbol denotes awareness).

The second loop continuously adjusts existing operations and processes to fit changing circumstances (just like a sunflower constantly adjusts itself to follow the sun across the sky). And the third loop provides agility for companies to create new processes and products to seize new opportunities (the leaping panther symbolizes agility).

The figure below illustrates how these three loops work together (it is excerpted from my book *Business Agility: Sustainable Prosperity in a Relentlessly Competitive World*). This isn't just a model for an agile IT organization, it is a model for an agile enterprise of any sort, business or technical. Think of how information technology in all its many forms and combinations can be employed to support the functioning of these three feedback loops in your company.

Exhibit 2.1 Three Feedback Loops Drive the Agile Organization

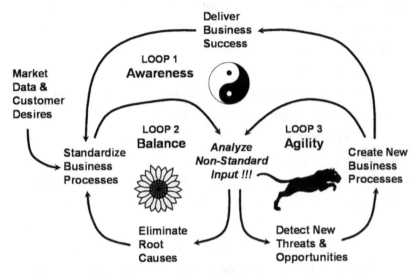

LOOP 1: **Awareness** = Monitoring and responding
LOOP 2: **Balance** = Improving existing processes
LOOP 3: **Agility** = Creating new processes

Loop 1 – Strategic Skills

Loop 1 encompasses environmental monitoring and responsive decision making. The people in this process are responsible for making the decisions that deliver successful IT alignment with the business. This is where CIOs focus most of their time because this is where they deliver the most value to their companies.

The focus of the environmental monitoring and decision making process must be to identify, analyze, and respond to the "non-standard inputs" as shown in Exhibit 2.1. This is because the most profitable opportunities for better alignment of IT and business often arise from agile responses to new or unexpected events (non-standard inputs). The CIO needs to know when transaction processing volumes increase or decrease at unexpected rates and when system processing or

21

operating errors occur at greater than expected rates. These events usually signify a need to improve an existing IT operation. The CIO also needs to know when new competitors enter the market and when sales of certain products increase or decrease faster than expected. Events like these often signify a need to create a new process.

For example, consider the response you would make to the unexpected news that sales of your company's new product X were increasing much faster than had been anticipated and also that customers who bought product X were two-thirds more likely to then purchase product Y within the following 60 days. The way you as the CIO respond to this unexpected news and the speed with which you do so will be a determining factor in how much success your company can achieve.

You need to consider the IT components that support product X and determine how to scale them up faster than originally planned to handle the extra sales volume. Then you need to decide what new IT support can enable the company to best exploit the emerging opportunity for sales of product Y and how soon that support should be in place.

In responding to this unexpected news you might decide to launch two projects. One project would accelerate the build-out of processing capacity for the systems that support product X. The other project would develop new systems to address the emerging opportunity for product Y and other follow-on product sales. Your level of agility will be measured by how appropriate your decisions are and how well you and your IT organization can carry them out.

After making a Loop 1 decision, one or both of the other two loops engage to act on the decision. Loop 2 focuses on improving existing operations – delivering efficiency. Loop 3 focuses on creating new operations – delivering effectiveness. When used in combination, the IT organization can use these three loops to sense changes and respond efficiently and effectively.

Loops 2 and 3 - Tactical Skills

A close examination of the agility process diagram reveals several important features of Loops 2 and 3 that contribute to an agile IT organization. First, notice that data from the environment and customer demands are handled by a set of standardized operating processes. They handle most of the input reliably and efficiently.

The IT systems that drive the standard operating processes (SOPs) of the company should be as automated and reliable as possible. They are the basic transaction processing systems such as ERP, order management, and production scheduling. Make them stable and scalable to handle the fluctuating transaction-processing loads required to support the company in performing its day-to-day operations. Give them robust error handling capabilities that prevent bad data from entering the company's systems. Identify, isolate and set aside bad data or "non-standard input" for appropriate people (not computers) to examine.

The agility of an IT organization is directly related to its ability to handle non-standard input. Automated transaction processing systems handle the standard input so people can focus on everything that is non-standard. This is where people bring the most value and where they should spend most of their time. People need to be skilled in analyzing non-standard input to determine its cause. Non-standard input comes from one of two conditions.

The first condition results from errors in the input data or in the system operations. If there are errors in the data or system operations people use Loop 2 to identify root causes of the errors to fix or improve the relevant standard operating processes and the systems that support them.

The second condition occurs when the input data is correct and it represents a new trend or an event that was not anticipated when the system was built. New events occur as business conditions and markets change and there are no standard operating procedures to deal with the occurrence. In this case, people use Loop 3 to make assessments about whether it represents a threat or an opportunity.

Their work often results in the creation of a new operating process in response to this form of non-standard input. If successful, the new process is added to the existing stack of standard operating processes. In this way the standard operating processes themselves continue to evolve as the company evolves – the agile process that maintains IT alignment.

Clearly, agile people in an agile IT organization must be skilled in the tasks called for by these three process loops. Let's take a more detailed look at each loop. First we will map out the activities that are involved and then we will discuss some of the tactical skills and technology needed to do these activities well.

Loop 1 – Monitoring and Deciding

Flying a jet fighter plane in combat is perhaps the epitome of agility. A fighter pilot named John Boyd devoted his life to understanding and teaching the skills of agility. He fought in the Korean War and then went on to became an instructor teaching the best U.S. and allied pilots in advanced air-to-air combat tactics.

Over the years he articulated what he had learned about the best way to deal with fast-paced and complex environments. Boyd encapsulated his teachings in a learnable and repeatable process that shows individuals and whole organizations how to compete and win in any high-change situation. He named this process "Observe – Orient – Decide – Act" (OODA) – also known as the OODA Loop or Boyd Cycle.

The monitoring and decision making activities of Loop 1 in the agility process are well described by the OODA Loop. The next sections describe the the OODA Loop and show how it can be applied to the operations of an IT organization.

Following the Four Steps

There are four steps in the OODA Loop, and the first step is to *observe*. This step involves collecting and communicating information about the environment. In an IT organization this includes information such as performance statistics for all systems, project status for all development work, and budgetary status.

The second step is to *orient*. This is the most important activity because it is where information is turned into understanding. Understanding is used to build an appreciation of the situation and its possibilities. The next two steps depend on this appreciation of the situation.

Translated in terms of an IT organization, the first and second steps mean that the IT operating environment is described and relevant measures are plotted over time so that performance trends become visible. The progress of the different system development projects are summarized showing key project completion statistics such as money spent, deliverables produced, and time and budget. These steps also lay out other expenses in areas such as systems operation, staff training, and salaries. With this information people can assess the situation and look for new threats and opportunities in the IT environment.

In the third step, *decide*, people (1) investigate different responses to threats and opportunities and (2) create and evaluate plans for implementing different responses. In an IT organization this means creation, evaluation, planning, and budgets for different system architectures and development projects. IT staff members consult with people from the business units who will be users of potential new systems.

Choosing the most appropriate plans leads to the fourth step – *act*. Depending on the decisions made in the orient and decide steps, the act step results in a tactical action that either improves an existing process (Loop 2) or creates a new process (Loop 3). In the act step, action is taken with either favorable, not favorable, or indeterminate results. These results are picked up in the observe step and the loop continues.

Note that the OODA Loop does not require people to cycle through all four steps all of the time. It is not a lock-step sequence. For example, the decide step is not needed when an environment is well understood. People can simply cycle quickly between orient and act steps in a series of rapid responses. At other times people may decide not to act at all but just observe and orient, waiting for an appropriate opportunity to act. It is better to think of the OODA Loop as an interactive network of activities with the orient step at its core instead of a fixed sequence of steps as illustrated in Exhibit 2.2.

Exhibit 2.2 The OODA Loop

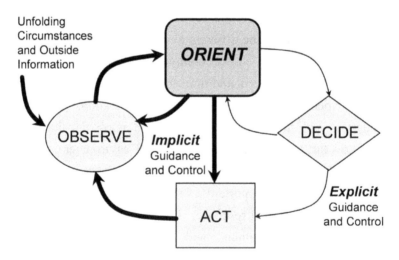

Orient is the Most Important Step

Let's take a closer look at the orient step since it is the most important. People form a picture of the world in the orient step, and this picture of the world drives the decisions and actions that follow. Good orientation is central to one's ability to take effective tactical action and achieve desirable results.

The orient step needs the most support from business intelligence (BI) capabilities. The real world unfolds in "an irregular, disorderly, unpredictable manner" as Colonel Boyd put it. Effective CIOs watch their business and IT environments and make decisions about how best to respond as day-to-day and week-to-week situations unfold. Dashboards and other Web-based reporting systems significantly improve outcomes in this step.

Another major concept of the OODA Loop implies that everyone in an agile organization has a common understanding of the organization's purpose and its major objectives. In military organizations this is known as the "commander's intent" or the "mission orders" – people are told what needs to be done but they are not told how to do it. They are not micromanaged; instead they are trusted to do the right thing.

The OODA Loop expresses common understanding of purpose with the notions of implicit guidance and explicit guidance. When the IT staff knows what the CIO expects of them and when they possess accurate, timely information about their own performance they take their own corrective actions as demanded by the situation.

If the CIO defines performance objectives for the IT organization and makes performance data available via dashboards and other BI systems then people do not need to be told what actions to take. They can see for themselves what the situation demands and they act appropriately. In this way the CIO provides implicit guidance to the IT organization. As shown by the heavier lines on the OODA Loop diagram, the best CIOs most often depend on implicit guidance.

CIOs provide explicit guidance when they make decisions to change IT strategy and stop or start IT development projects. CIOs use explicit guidance when the rules of the game change. When this happens people need to be informed of the changes and told how those changes affect their jobs and performance expectations. Once this happens people readjust, and implicit guidance again takes over to guide their actions.

As the CIO you need to make sure that you clearly explain what you expect of people in your organization. You need to define clear performance measures. When people know what you expect of them and when they get regular and accurate performance reports then implicit guidance works very well. Implicit guidance is more efficient than explicit guidance because it requires less of the CIO's time once the performance expectations are in place.

Some combination of three leadership errors is troubling your IT organization if you always have to tell people what to do and how to do it: (1) You may not have clearly defined your expectations; (2) People are not getting timely performance reports; (3) You may be changing your mind and starting new projects too frequently.

These three leadership errors push the CIO into excessive use of explicit guidance practices. People cannot be agile in an explicit guidance environment. They are always waiting for the CIO to make decisions and tell them what to do. If you constantly resort to explicit guidance practices to get things done in your IT organization then you must find ways to address the reasons causing this unhealthy situation. Your organization cannot be agile until you address these issues.

Depending on the decisions people make in the orient and decide steps, an IT organization is constantly called on to act. At the highest level, action can be thought of as activities that fall into one of two categories. The first category includes tactical activities that improve existing operations (Loop 2). The second category includes activities that create something new (Loop 3).

Loop 2: Improving Existing Processes

In addition to being a universally applicable performance measurement, six sigma provides milestones as IT organizations and project teams move through the activities they need to improve their operations and their products (see Sidebar). A five-step process guides IT teams through these six sigma activities: define, measure, analyze, improve, and control. The process is shown in Exhibit 2.3. It is known as DMAIC (first letter of each step) and is pronounced "dee-MAY-ic". Let's take a look at the activities in each step.

Exhibit 2.3 Steps in Six Sigma DMAIC Process

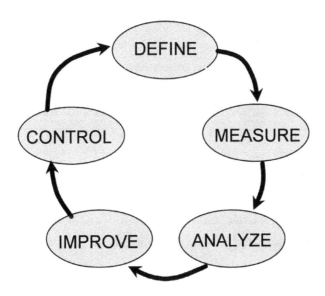

Define - Most of the CIO's work begins with definitions. The define step begins a six sigma project and produces three important documents. The first document is the project charter. The charter lays out the business case and the problem statement. It also clearly defines the project scope so that the project team knows exactly where to focus and what they should avoid. The charter also articulates the goal or mission of the project and the specific objectives that the team needs to achieve in order to accomplish the goal. Operationally, the charter lays out project milestones that indicate to the team where and when they should be achieving other sequential steps in the DMAIC process. Finally, the charter describes the roles and responsibilities of the team members, the team leader, and the project executive sponsor.

In addition to the project charter, the second document produced in this step defines and documents the customers that will be served and their needs and expectations. The needs and expectations of the customers tell the team what to measure and improve. The third document is a high-level process map that shows the tasks involved in the process and the inputs and outputs of each task. The high-level process map shows everyone involved with the project the exact sequence of tasks that are candidates for improvement.

Measure - In this step the project team creates a data collection plan and then collects data that measures the current state of the process or product targeted for improvement. The data collected reflects customer requirements and shows how often the process actually meets customer requirements. The data also shows the activity levels of key tasks in the process.

After collecting the data the team calculates the existing sigma measurement for the process. This obvious step of collecting data and documenting the current situation is often overlooked or done poorly because the project team thinks they already know what is wrong and they want to get on to fixing the problem. Good data collection gets the project off to a start in the right direction.

Analyze - In this step the project team applies statistical analysis tools to discover and validate root causes of problems. Many of the tools used in this step come from total quality management. The team uses cause and effect diagrams and frequency distribution charts to pinpoint the sources of error in the process being investigated. They use scatter diagrams to test the strength of correlations between one variable and another in the process. They use run charts to track the performance patterns of various tasks and of the process overall.

As they pinpoint problems, the team then formulates options for eliminating or reducing these problems and compares the different options. How difficult is each option? How much will each cost? What impact will each option have on improving the sigma measure of the process?

Improve - In this step the team leader works with the project's executive sponsor to select a group of improvement options. They choose the options with the best chance for success and with the greatest impact on the process.

With the sponsor's backing, the DMAIC team implements the selected improvements to the process. Best practice calls for the team to implement the improvements one at a time or in small groups of related improvements. After implementing each improvement the team should collect process performance data and recalculate the sigma measure – hopefully the sigma measure improves. Recollection and recalculation ensures that either the improvements actually provide valuable results or they are discontinued.

Control - One a team makes process improvements they need to regularly monitor the process to assure that the improvements stay in place and remain effective. The DMAIC project team defines a set of measurements collected on an on-going basis to document performance levels of the improved process.

In addition, the team creates a response plan that lays out corrective actions if on-going performance measures indicate that the improvements are beginning to slip. Over the longer term, the greatest benefit from the six sigma approach is that organizations reap the very real benefits of process improvements that continue to improve and thus deliver more and more value.

Loop 3: Creating New Processes

IT executives can use agility to boost innovation. An innovative process calls for people to feel a sense of urgency in order to overcome the inertia of doing things the same old way. So placing limits on the time and money that your employees can spend to solve a problem is a great way to create urgency. We are not talking about doing things on the cheap. We are talking about doing them faster and smarter. Challenge yourself and your staff to innovate solutions that cost 10 times less than what our competition is spending and that can be deployed four times faster–call it "10/4 performance."

Agility and innovation starts with a frame of mind, and that frame of mind is embodied in a simple three-step process called "Define-Design-Build." It's a simple, easily understood process that guides people through the three steps of developing any new system or business process.

Each step produces a well-defined set of deliverables and uses tight time boxes for how much time to allocate to each step. See Exhibit 2.4. This process guides your innovation and agility and it can be cycled through every 30-60-90 days depending on the size of the development project, the urgency of the project, and other considerations. We'll discuss this further in Chapter 4.

Exhibit 2.4 Agility & Innovation in a Three-Step Process

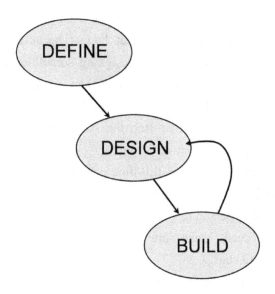

The key here is to remember that regardless of the times you choose, this is an iterative approach that does not try to solve all problems at once. Instead you focus on developing solutions to the most pressing problems first and get those solutions into operation. Then you iterate again and add additional features as needed. Then keep iterating and adding more features as needed.

Agility Means Move It or Lose

The Define step takes 2 weeks (or on an agile project can be accelerated to 2 days) and typically costs 5 to 10 percent of the total project budget. The Design step takes 1 month (or accelerated to 7 days) and costs 15 to 30 percent of the total budget. And the Build phase takes 2 months (or accelerated to 13 days) and costs 60 to 80 percent of the total budget.

You may ask, "How do we know these time frames without knowing the specifics of a given project?" Simply put, there is only that much time available if you are truly going to be agile. If people can't define what is needed within two to six weeks, then it certainly won't be an agile project. Likewise, we know the design work will only cost 15 to 30 percent of the total project budget because if people are spending more than that, they are designing something too complex. More expensive projects will take longer than one to three months to design and then will take too long to build. In sum, if the work cannot meet these requirements, then stop the project because whatever is being done is neither innovative nor agile.

Every project needs a full-time person in charge who has the skills and authority to get things done and is totally committed to success. I call that person the "system builder". Without that person, no project can succeed. Make sure you have good system builders for every project you start.

Next, build robust 80 percent solutions rather than attempting to build 100 percent solutions. Avoid the temptation to over-engineer your systems in an attempt to handle every possible combination of events. Trying to build systems that can handle everything increases the cost and complexity in an exponential fashion. Have people, not computers, handle the exceptions and the one-off occurrences, and develop systems to handle only the routine, day-in, day-out transactions. This is how you build systems for 10 times less than your competition.

Remember that big systems are always composed of a collection of smaller subsystems. So once the Define step is completed, big, multimillion-dollar projects can be broken up into smaller projects to develop each subsystem. Instead of one big project team designing everything and then building everything, this arrangement allows multiple smaller teams to design and build subsystems in parallel, under the overall direction of the system builder. This is how to get things done four times faster than your competition.

At first people may accuse executives who adopt a process such as Define-Design-Build of being overly demanding and unreasonable. But do not relent. What you ask is possible–development groups can achieve 10/4 performance levels. Give people the training they need and opportunities to learn by doing, but do not lower your standards or extend the time frames.

Dynamics of the Agile IT Organization

The concept of management by exception is nothing new, but in the context of the agile IT organization it is absolutely central to the way the organization works. The agile IT organization lives in a world of continuous and enormous flows of data. How does it process this data without becoming overwhelmed? The agile IT organization works by using standardized operating procedures (in effect an autonomic nervous system) that handles all routine transactions automatically with little or no human intervention. The organization devotes most of its peoples' time (its conscious nervous system) to handling only the exceptions or the non-standard inputs.

In an agile IT organization automated business process management (BPM) systems immediately notify appropriate people when exceptions or non-standard input occur. People analyze exceptions, not computers. If there are errors in the data, people track down root causes and fix them.

When the data is not in error but indicates the appearance of something new, it is very important to have people in the exception-handling loop. This puts them in immediate and intimate contact with the data indicating a change that could be an emerging threat or opportunity. Using implicit guidance they make decisions and act quickly. If changes of strategy are needed, the CIO gets involved and issues explicit guidance. Exhibit 2.5 illustrates the system dynamics of the agile IT organization. ∞

Exhibit 2.5 System Dynamics of the Agile IT Organization

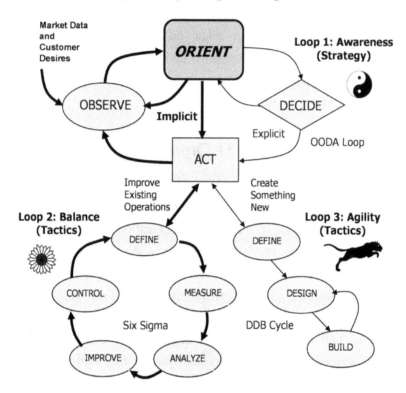

Notes and Ideas for Action:

Notes and Ideas for Action:

Chapter 3.

Core Techniques for Agility

This section takes a look at the application of the six core techniques and how their use drives the Define-Design-Build process. Every CIO must be familiar with these techniques. Although CIOs do not perform the actual work of developing new systems, they must be conversant with the proper application of these core techniques to lead their organizations effectively.

Just as the game of basketball relies on use of techniques such as dribbling, passing, and shooting, the game of developing information systems depends on its own set of basic techniques. The CIO can objectively measure the skill levels of IT project teams by how capably team members apply these techniques. By skillfully applying these techniques in combinations most appropriate to different situations, an agile project team can always produce competent – and sometimes even brilliant - results. CIOs must see to it that their people are trained in these techniques and that every project team has people skilled in applying the right mix of these techniques to succeed with their project.

Just a Handful of Techniques

The activities in each of the three steps can be accomplished by using an appropriate combination of just a few of techniques. I call this small set the "core techniques" because they are the basic techniques that every systems developer should understand and be able to use. Regardless of the specific technology being used and regardless of the specific business process being addressed, these core techniques remain relevant and applicable. The set of six core techniques are:

1) Joint Applications Design – an inclusive process that combines ideas from both business and technical people to create new system designs.

2) Process Mapping – exploring and mapping out business work flows.

3) Data Modeling – defining the data used by business work flows.

4) System Prototyping – a way to model and validate both the user interface and the technical architecture of a system.

5) Object Oriented Design & Programming – designing and specifying the structure and working logic of software that will be created.

6) System Test & Roll Out – testing, training, and implementation of new systems.

These techniques are well known in the IT profession so training and reference material are widely available. People on project teams must be able to apply an appropriate combination of these techniques as needed within the time boxes defined for each step of the Define-Design-Build process. Combinations of the core techniques create the agile tactics needed to develop systems within the short timeframes required to support organizations in high change environments.

Joint Application Design

The joint application design or JAD is a structured brainstorming technique that enables a project leader to create an inclusive process that brings together the knowledge and insights of all the team members. The JAD techniques lay down a set of rules that govern how the team leader leads, how team members interact, and how the team approaches problems. These rules stimulate the creative problem solving abilities of the team and allow the team to generate a stream of ideas that then become the raw material from which the system design emerges.

JAD is a direct response to the overwhelming complexity of the design tasks that we face in business today. People individually analyzing parts of a problem either alone or in isolated groups cannot develop competent or adequate system designs on a consistent basis. However, using the JAD rules, project teams with the appropriate mix of business and technical people can come up with competent system designs every time. A basic set of JAD ground rules is listed below. And the JAD process is illustrated in Exhibit 3.1.

> *Attendance of all team members is expected* - If any team member cannot be at a JAD session then reschedule the session.

> *Check you baggage at the door* - Everyone has a stack of problems and personal issues. Leave them out of the JAD session.

> *Start and end sessions on time* - Everyone is busy these days so treat the time spent in JAD sessions as valuable and respect people's schedules.

Every session must have an agenda - At the beginning of each session review and confirm the list of issues the group will address and the deliverables it will create.

Everyone is of equal rank while in the JAD session - Everyone on the team is equally important in what they have to contribute or else they would not have been asked to participate.

Team member comments will be kept confidential - In order to participate freely, people must know that statements they may make will not be repeated outside the session to people who could hurt or embarrass them.

Deal with issues not personalities - We can discuss issues and evaluate solutions to them in a rational and creative way only if we ourselves are not personally being discussed or evaluated.

Everyone participates, no side conversations - It is through the combined insights and ideas of the whole group that good ideas emerge. Side conversations are distracting and disrespectful to the group.

Reach consensus or request "a decision from above" - If the JAD team cannot come to an agreement on a particular issue, then it must outline several possible solutions and ask for a decision from the executive sponsor of the project.

Exhibit 3.1 Joint Application Design

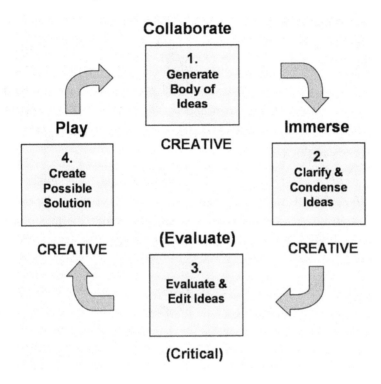

Collaboration teams of business and technical people produce better ideas than people working on their own

CREATIVE thinking must come before critical thinking!

Keep critical thinking separate from creative thinking or nothing will happen (creative thinking is hard, don't let it get bogged down with critical thinking)

Process Mapping

Process mapping defines a set of steps for identifying the work processes that occur in a company and the connections between these processes. The team first identifies the highest-level processes and then the sub-processes within each high level process. They define the data inputs required by each process and list the sources of the data. Their work also defines data outputs generated by each process and lists the destinations of the data outputs.

This technique uses diagrams to create a visual map of the tasks in any process and the data that flows between the tasks. This visual map creates a common reference framework for business and technical people to discuss issues and discover opportunities for process improvements. Process maps are far more effective than written documents because they use graphic means to communicate a lot of information quickly and accurately. Exhibit 3.2 shows an example of a process map diagram.

Exhibit 3.2 Process Map

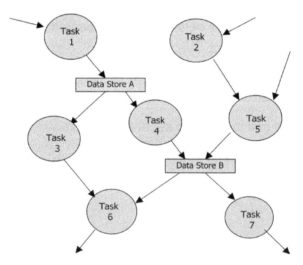

The process map shows the inputs and outputs of tasks in the workflow. It may also show places where data is stored.

Data Modeling

The data model defines the entities about which data needs to be collected. The entities are usually identified while using the process mapping technique. Entities such as customer, product, and invoice can be found in the data flows between different business processes. The data model then defines the properties or attributes that must be known about an entity. For example the entity called "customer" has attributes such as customer number, name, address, and credit limit.

Data modeling also produces a visual diagram called an entity-relationship diagram or ERD. Like the process flow diagrams produced by the process mapping technique, the ERDs provide another visual method for communicating a lot of information to the business and technical members of a project team. Everyone on a team can spot-check the entities on the diagram with which they are most familiar to ensure accuracy. Exhibit 3.3 shows an example of an entity relationship diagram.

Exhibit 3.3 Data Model – Entity Relationship Diagram

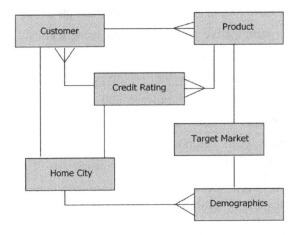

This sample data model shows that there are six entities that a certain business process needs to know about and how these entities relate to each other.

System Prototyping

There are two kinds of system prototyping. The first kind of system prototype is a system's user interface model. By looking at the process mapping diagrams the project team decides which tasks will be fully automated, which ones will be a mix of human activity supported by a computer, and which ones will be completely done by humans. And by looking at the data model they can see what data will be handled by each task.

The prototype of the user interface builds upon this knowledge to create the layout and sequence of computer screens to support the tasks where humans and computers interact. The user interface prototype also illustrates how the users of the system can navigate between screens, and it shows the layout of any printed output generated by the system.

The development team designs this kind of prototype by using an interactive slide show displayed on a computer screen that allows the system user to move from one screen to another via keyboard, mouse, or other commands. It shows the business people what they will get when the new system is built. The interface prototype is something tangible and participative that people can work with, respond to, and make suggestions for improvement.

The second kind of system prototype is a technical architecture prototype composed of the hardware and software components that have been selected to build the system. This prototype demonstrates how well the system components will work together. The selected software is installed on the selected hardware. Links are then established between the different software components. The team passes data back and forth under different conditions to measure the hardware and software components' ability to work together and handle the expected number of users and volumes of data.

The architectural prototype shows the technical people what issues they will face when they build the system. It allows people to verify that the technology they have proposed to use in building the system will work as advertised and meet the performance demands of the new system. Exhibit 3.4 illustrates the idea of the two types of system prototypes – the technical architecture and the user interface.

Exhibit 3.4 System Prototype

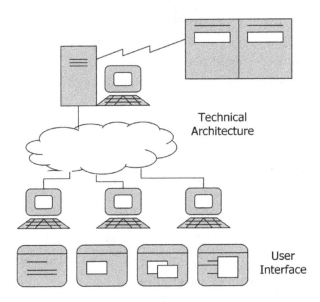

Technical Architecture

User Interface

The prototype of the system's user interface shows how people will use the system. The prototype of the system's technical architecture shows how the system will be built.

Object Oriented Design & Programming

Object oriented design (OOD) and object oriented programming (OOP) are the latest incarnation of a set of techniques that have been evolving for the last 30 years in the systems building profession. The purpose of these techniques is to enable the design and programming of stable, reusable software that is easy to debug and easy to modify.

The object-oriented techniques are analogous to the engineering techniques an electrical engineer uses when designing a piece of equipment such as a cellular phone. The cell phone is specified as a collection of component parts. Many of these parts are integrated circuit chips (IC chips) plugged into a motherboard. Each IC chip is defined by the inputs it accepts, the operations it performs, and the output it creates.

Software objects are the equivalent of the IC chip in this example. A system is composed of interacting software objects just as a cell phone is composed of interacting IC chips. The popular technique of Web services is an example of object-oriented programming. Web services are composed of programs (objects) from existing systems that communicate with each other by sending inputs and receiving outputs over the Internet using agreed upon XML formats.

Once the object-oriented design has been completed, the programming is a relatively straightforward process of writing code to meet the design specifications for each object. All the hard decisions about how the objects operate and interact to drive the system are made in the object-oriented design. The choice of the programming language influences the design of the objects to some extent, but the object design is largely language independent.

The system builder can manage the programming effort very effectively by simply tracking the programming progress object by object. Generally, objects can be programmed in one to three days. They can be programmed in any order and could all be done in parallel if there are enough programmers available. In this way, new programmers can be added to speed up the programming process without causing confusion and loss of project control. Exhibit 3.5 illustrates a sample object model diagram.

Exhibit 3.5 Object Model

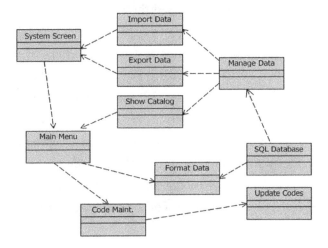

The object model shows the modules of program code - the objects – and how these objects interact with each other to drive the system.

System Test & Roll Out

Project teams use these techniques to test the system in a thorough and orderly manner to find and fix the bugs and then to roll the system into production. System test and roll out techniques allow people on the project teams to first test each object individually, then to test the groups of objects used in each system function, and finally to test the entire system.

The developers who program each object first perform unit testing on the object. When an object passes the unit test, it is checked into a system test environment. People familiar with the specific operations that the system is designed to perform create test scripts and use these test scripts to put different parts of the system through its paces. They write test scripts that exercise the different features of the system in a wide range of usage scenarios. The entire system is assembled and tested as more and more parts of the system come

49

together in the test environment. This is known as test-driven development.

Once the system has passed through the test environment with all the bugs fixed, the team follows a regular sequence in rolling out the system. The first step uses a beta test or pilot group of people who begin using the system for their normal jobs. The pilot group participants define a range of system modifications that fine-tune the operation of the system and improve the ease with which it can be used.

Finally, the system rolls into production. Appropriate training always anticipates and supports the roll into production so that people who depend on the system are not left to cope with the change entirely on their own. The system testing sequence is illustrated in Exhibit 3.6.

Exhibit 3.6 System Testing Sequence

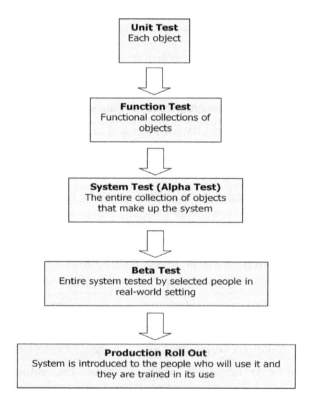

Tactical Principles for Running Projects

Once strategy has been defined, the game is all about tactics. The execution of any strategy depends on the effective use of tactics. Our profession has had enough experience by now to know that there is a right way to run projects, and the CIO is responsible for insuring that development teams use appropriate tactics. Every CIO should understand and use a short list of six tactical principles. These principles apply whenever the CIO and IT organization perform development work to deliver a new system or enhance an existing system.

Appropriate project tactics follow these six principles, and there is no convincing reason to violate any of these principles. Follow these principles and you can tailor specific tactics for any project and enjoy consistently good results. Ignore any one of them and you undermine the effectiveness of the others - so use them all.

1. Every Project needs a full time leader with overall responsibility and the appropriate authority – the system builder. There must be a single person who is responsible for the project's success who is totally focused on getting the job done. This person must also have the authority within the project to make decisions and act quickly without having to get permission from senior management.

System builders always appreciate having the backup of a steering committee or management oversight group to which they report, but a committee cannot make decisions in a timely manner. If a qualified system builder is not in place the progress and cost of the project will reflect the absence of such a person – progress will be slow and costs will be high.

2. Define a set of measurable and non-overlapping objectives that are necessary and sufficient to accomplish the project goal or mission. It is crucial that you define clear project objectives so that the people who are assigned the responsibility to achieve these objectives know what is expected of them. It is very important that the boundaries of these objectives do not overlap because if they do, the overlap will cause confusion and conflict between the teams assigned to achieve these overlapping objectives.

Make sure that each objective is absolutely necessary to the accomplishment of the project goal. Do not pursue an objective just because it seems like a good idea. Finally, you must be able to say that the mission or goal will be accomplished when all objectives have been achieved. The objectives must cover everything that needs to happen.

3. Assign project objectives to teams of 2-7 people with hands-on team leaders and the appropriate mix of business and technical skills. Put together a project team of two to seven people who in your judgment have among them the necessary business and technical skills and experience to address the issues that you expect to arise in achieving the objectives you delegate to them. A team is a self-organizing group of people with complementary skills such that all members contribute their strengths without being penalized for their weaknesses. Each member of the team concentrates on the aspects of designing and building the system that they are best at and/or most interested in.

A properly configured team enables the team leader to delegate tasks to people who are interested in these tasks. People spend most or all of their time doing tasks they are interested in and little or no time doing tasks they are not interested in. Within a team, the operative word is "we," not "me". The whole team is rewarded for successes and takes responsibility for mistakes. Singling out superstars or scapegoats undermines team moral and performance.

4. Tell the teams WHAT to do but not HOW to do it. Point a project team in the right direction by giving them a well-defined project goal and clearly identify the project objectives for which they are responsible. The objectives define the outcomes that they must deliver to be successful. The project goal and the objectives that you delegate to a team defines the game that you want that team to play. The team itself must then go through the process of creating their plan to achieve the objectives that you have defined for them.

General Patton said, " Tell people what you want but don't tell them how to do it – you will be surprised by their resourcefulness in accomplishing their tasks." The teams can make changes or additions to the objectives they are given as long as you and they agree that the modified objectives are still necessary and sufficient to accomplish the project goal.

5. Break project work into tasks that are each a week or less in duration and produce something of value to the business every 30 – 90 days. Encourage project teams to structure their project plans so that each task can be accomplished within a week or less and has a well defined deliverable. Track these tasks as either started, delayed, or finished. Do not fall into the trap of tracking tasks by their percentage of completion as it is unclear what "percent complete" really means. Delivering tasks on time is the key deliverable.

The system builder must be able to track progress at the task level of detail in order to keep accurate projections of the time to complete and the cost to complete for each of the project's objectives. Multi-week tasks make progress hard to measure, and they are the ones that suddenly surprise the system builder. Multi-week tasks reported by the percent complete method often seem to show good progress, but then in the last week they suddenly turn out to be nowhere near completion.

Project tasks should combine to produce something that is of value to the business every 30 to 90 days. This provides the opportunity for the business to verify that the project is on the right track. It also provides deliverables that the business can start to use even before the entire project is complete and begin to see some return the cost of the project.

6. Every project needs project office staff to work with the system builder and team leaders to update plans and budgets. The project plan and budget are analogous to the profit and loss statements for a business. They must be updated continuously and accurately in order to provide the people running the project with the information they need to make good decisions. There is a common but misguided notion that the system builder and team leaders should be the ones who keep the plans updated. This is analogous to the idea that the president of a company and its managers should spend their time keeping the company's books.

Just as there is an accounting department to keep the company's books, there needs to be a project office group that keeps the projects plans and budgets current. The project office staff reports to the system builder and works with the team leaders on a weekly basis to review and update the plans and budgets associated with each team objectives. In this way the system builder can accurately monitor project progress and the team leaders are able to focus on running their teams rather than filling out reports. (See Exhibit 3.7)

Exhibit 3.7 Tactical Principles for Driving Projects

Tactical Principles
for Running Projects

1. Every project needs a full time leader with overall responsibility and authority.

2. Define a set of measurable and non-overlapping objectives that are necessary and sufficient to accomplish the project goal or mission.

3. Assign project objectives to teams of 2-7 people with hands-on team leaders and the appropriate mix of business and technical skills.

4. Tell the teams WHAT to do but not HOW to do it.

5. Break project work into tasks that are each a week or less in duration and produce something of value to the business every 30 – 90 days.

6. Provide project office staff to work with the project leader and team leaders to update plans and budgets.

Agile Project Management

People on agile projects need a "Big Picture" that shows them what's happening every day. Much has been said about the evils of Gantt charts and the oppressive and bureaucratic project management procedures that often come with them. I feel the pain of those who echo these sentiments, yet I caution people about not throwing the baby out with the bathwater.

You can't run a project bigger than three people for longer than three weeks with just To-Do Lists. On bigger projects people need to see the whole picture. They need to see how their tasks relate to tasks everybody else is doing and what will happen if certain tasks take longer to get done or if new tasks are added. Everybody on an agile project team needs to see clearly every day what's happening and who's doing what so people can coordinate with each other effectively. Without visibility there is no agility.

As we talk, we start sketching out that big picture called a project plan. We define five main objectives that are necessary and sufficient to accomplish the mission (which is to roll out the first production version of the system in early May). We decide to iteratively build the system in two 30-day iterations (we could call these 30-day iterations Blitzes; see more about this in Chapter 4) and frontload most of the development work into the first iteration so we have time in the second blitz to fine tune functions as needed and shift from the tasks of developing software to the tasks of rolling that software into production.

Objectives are specific, measurable actions that can be objectively measured as either done or not done. A project plan starts with a set of five to seven objectives that are necessary and sufficient to accomplish the project mission. If you have a list of 20 objectives then nobody can remember what they are so the plan is too complex to be useful. And if you look at a list of 20 objectives you'll find most of them are actually subtasks within a few higher level objectives.

For each objective we list out the high level tasks for the work needed to achieve that objective. Then we set task durations and dependencies between tasks and assign people to each task. No task has a fixed start or finish date; they only have durations and dependencies; only exception is for the very first tasks in a project plan that have no earlier dependent tasks. These first tasks are assigned start dates and every other task starts as dictated by its dependencies. The plan created this way is fluid and reflects changes as they happen (and all plans do change, if they don't it means they're not real). Changes instantly ripple through the plan as tasks and dependencies are added or modified like what happens when you type in new numbers on a spreadsheet; changes ripple throughout the spreadsheet and everybody can see the effects of those changes right away.

As much as possible, we arrange to run work on each objective in parallel with the other objectives so slowdowns on work for one objective don't hold up work on other objectives. And within objectives, we also arrange tasks to run in parallel as much as possible. Stair step patterns of task sequences are dangerous because a delay in one task starts pushing all following tasks farther and farther out creating a cascading effect that is hard to get back under control.

When defining relationships between tasks the classic "finish to start" relationship between one task and another is what creates the stair step pattern. Strive instead to define tasks that have "finish to finish" relationships between them. That means you can run them in parallel.

Each objective gets its own section in the project plan and within the section for each objective we lay out the high level activities to design and build the deliverables called for by each objective. You can see the first 30-Day Blitz got the most tasks and details; that's because we know more about the near term than we do about the longer term and there's no point in pretending we know more than we do. Once there is a first version project plan in place, then people can further break apart each high level task and add more detail as it becomes clearer.

Exhibit 3.8 Project Plan Showing Blitzes

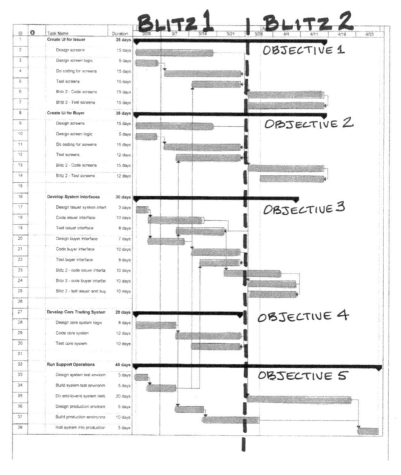

This is just the first iteration of the project plan. The plan will unfold and more detail will be added each day as more detail can be defined. The overall time boxes for each objective will remain the same though. So as high level tasks are further defined and more low level detail tasks are added there is a process of ongoing adjustment to get things done within the time and resource constraints of the project. Additional tasks are not simply added on in leisurely stair-step sequences that push final completion further and further out. Agility is about maneuvering within constraints to get things done. This is a demanding discipline. It calls for creativity to get things done quickly and simply and it pushes people to focus on doing only the most important things.

A project plan is a set of tasks with time boxes and dependencies that create a desired deliverable. If those time boxes start to look like Gantt Charts then so be it... there's nothing intrinsically evil or oppressive about Gantt charts (even if we use something like Microsoft Project to generate those Gantt charts).

Five Questions Everyone Needs to Answer Every Day

In some quarters there is a misperception about the planning and coordination required for agile development. Often people new to agility have the impression that agility means it's just "runnin' and gunnin'" and you don't need to plan and manage the project. Actually what makes agility possible is more planning, more coordination and more visibility into what's happening than you would normally use on a traditional waterfall style development project.

The reason you need more planning and coordination is because there isn't much slack built into agile projects and things happen much more quickly than on a traditional project. The project team needs a continuously updated project plan showing daily progress at the detailed task level in order to stay on top of things. That means the project plan is updated every day not just once a week.

No project plan survives contact with reality. Things will not happen the way you think they will. As the project progresses, new tasks get added to the plan, other tasks get removed or updated, and task dependencies change constantly. Without an accurate and current plan, people on the project loose track of what's really going on and soon the cumulative impact of changing tasks and dependencies gets out of hand. Unexpected news starts arriving with increasing frequency and there is little time to act effectively. The team gets pushed into a mode of reacting to one unpleasant surprise after another. That's not agile; that's a death spiral.

To counteract this and keep the project plan current and clear use these five questions every day in the morning standup meetings. These questions are simple and they are yes/no questions. There is no room for answers like, "Yes but..." or that famous answer I hear from people who don't want to commit, "Yes and no..." Here are the five questions:

1. Has the scope of any project task changed? (Yes/No)

2. Will any major activity or milestone date be missed? (Yes/No)

3. Does the project team need any outside skills/expertise? (Yes/No)

4. Are there any unsolved technical problems? (Yes/No)

5. Are there any unresolved user review/approval problems? (Yes/No)

For all questions marked Yes, explain the problem and recommend possible solution(s)

The first question gets to the issue that things change as you find out more about them. Sometimes a task winds up requiring more work than you thought (and sometimes it turns out to be easier than you thought). When it takes more work add those additional tasks to the plan and add the durations for those tasks and their dependencies on other tasks in the plan. When doing this the team needs to see what it does to the final completion date of the project iteration or sprint (or blitz). This often requires the team to find simpler ways to do things or to make decisions about what tasks and system features can be deferred to a later iteration in order to deliver a working and viable system in the time available on the current iteration.

Regarding the second question, tasks on the plan are broken down to a level of detail where tasks are typically between a half day to two days long, and tasks are recorded as either started, finished, or delayed. There is none of that percent complete stuff (can anyone say what 70% complete actually means?). A task is deemed finished only when the task deliverable can be seen by the whole project team. If a task is delayed, the extra time needed to finish it is added to the task duration so everyone can see the effect that has on the project plan.

The third question makes sure that new tasks or other project developments are also seen in light of the new skill sets that might be needed because of those changes. The last thing an agile project needs is for people to try to learn a new skill or figure out a new piece of technology while also trying to get things done quickly.

The fourth question makes sure that people don't struggle all on their own with some problem. It works much better when people pool their collective wisdom to solve problems that come up. And the fifth question addresses a similar situation where a system user may disagree with a change the agile development team makes or may change their mind about what they want. Again there is no point in one team member struggling with that all on their own.

Exhibit 3.9 shows an example of how a project plan evolves from week to week on an agile project. You can see it gets longer as more things are discovered and more detail tasks are added to the plan.

Exhibit 3.9 Project Plans Expand as Detail is Added over Time

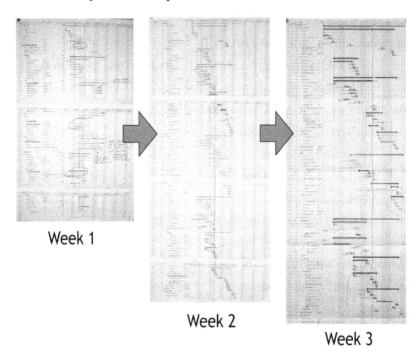

Week 1

Week 2

Week 3

The project plan and related story boards and status boards are living things. Project plans are the big picture view of the overall project and its progress and they gain more and more detail as the project progresses. Because the plan is always up to date and accurately reflecting progress and expectations on the project, it gives everybody a clear picture of what is happening so they can work together to solve problems that arise.

It also gives senior managers who are not on the project (but who are still ultimately responsible for what happens) the information they need to feel comfortable. And that saves project team members from being distracted by endless management questions and misplaced advice that is not helpful because nothing kills agility faster than endless management questions and misplaced advice. This is exactly the management dynamic that kills agility. ∞

Notes and Ideas for Action:

Notes and Ideas for Action:

Chapter 4.

The Agile 30-Day Blitz

The process of creating new IT systems has traditionally been described by various development methodologies. The problem with most development methodologies is that they are complex and often too cumbersome to apply in real life. An agile IT organization needs an agile process for developing new systems and enhancing existing ones. The process described here is based on the Agile Scrum methodology that has become so popular in the agile development world. I have field tested it over the years and refined it as I went. I call it the Agile 30-Day Blitz and it is particularly well suited for use by organizations just starting out with agile development. The 30-Day Blitz is simple, structured and iterative. It is designed to help people more quickly understand and apply agile development techniques.

Agile development processes have to be powerful yet simple enough so that people can understand and use them when they need them. They should also be flexible enough so that they can be tailored to meet the demands of any specific development challenge. The Define-Design-Build development process addresses these needs.

When you think about what is needed to create something new it all boils down to just three basic steps. First you need to define what you are going to create. Then you need to design how you will create it. And then you need to build it.

You can further divide each of these three steps into sub-steps, but this only increases the complexity of the process and reduces the likelihood that people will understand or use it effectively. Define-Design-Build provides an uncomplicated framework to guide development work for any new business process or system. It also provides a reliable way to estimate development times and budgets.

Benefits of Define-Design-Build Cycle

From the perspective of the CIO and other senior executives who sponsor a system development project, Define – Design - Build is a way to manage project risk. In the define phase small amounts of time and money are spent up front to qualify a business opportunity – 5-10% of the total project cost.

If findings warrant, the company then spends only a moderate amount of further time and money in design – 15-30% of the total project cost. In the design phase, a small, prototype system is created to prove that the opportunity is real and justifies a larger investment.

The build phase is where companies spend the most of the time and money– 60-80% of the project total. Notice that the decision to move into the build phase is made with the greatest amount of information. The nature of the business opportunity and the solution system that will exploit that opportunity are well established by that time.

From the perspective of the project leaders (the system builders), Define – Design - Build provides a way to navigate through the complexity of creating a new computer system. The system builder is truly the person on the hot seat who needs to get things done. The CIO and system builder use the Define – Design - Build process in combination with the strategic system design guidelines and the tactical principles for running projects (see Chapter 1) to structure the work sequence. The process lets them set reasonable time limits within which to investigate situations and make decisions in the Define and Design phases.

After making decisions about system design and budget, this same framework provides a set of tactics for the system builder and the team leaders to employ during the build phase. Core techniques employed in the build phase give structure to the work and enable the system builder to effectively focus and lead the effort.

From the perspective of the people on the project team Define – Design - Build is a clearly defined and manageable repertoire of techniques for completing new projects. People who participate in each of the three project phases know which of the core techniques they will be expected to use as the project move toward completion. They can focus on mastering these techniques. The CIO should emphasize that IT staff members work together on tasks in small groups so that the learning and use of techniques among team members is more effective than if they worked alone.

Coping with Complexity

Define – Design – Build is a three-step sequence that could also be described as, "Move it! Move it! Move it!" In order to support an agile IT organization in a high-change world, systems must be built with a quick and iterative process. The project team must strictly adhere to the time boxes for each step in the development sequence.

Complexity is as much perception as it is reality, and a disciplined, fast-paced approach is the best way to handle complexity. When the CIO allows project teams too much time to contemplate the situations facing them team members begin to perceive excessive amounts of complexity and sink into that dreaded state called "analysis paralysis".

Agility means learning to deal effectively with complexity. People learn to become agile when guided by a discipline for developing new systems in a fluid and coordinated manner. They learn by participating in project teams with people trained to use the Define – Design - Build process.

Define opportunities, design systems to exploit those opportunities, and quickly build those systems. As success with one opportunity opens up other opportunities, address each new opportunity using and refining the Define – Design - Build process. Your IT organization will build great credibility and momentum in this way.

Time-Boxing

The Define-Design-Build process depends heavily on the use of appropriate time boxes for getting things done in each of the three steps. Agile processes need to be quick. Regardless of the task at hand, an agile response must be a fast response. Time-boxing sets limits to the amount of time that can be spent on a task, and the job is shaped to fit within the constraints of that box.

Time-boxing helps keep a project moving along at a brisk pace. As the saying goes, "The job will expand to fill the time available." Therefore we respond to that tendency with time-boxed constraints on all development activities. Allocate only a certain amount of time and money to each of the three steps. People will learn to manage the scope and pace of the work to meet their due dates and budgets. Set the scope and pace of work in each step of the project to conform to the time and budget constraints shown in Exhibit 4.1.

If a step in the sequence is not completed in a timely manner, the process and the project itself is in danger of breaking down. People must stay on track. These constraints provide the implicit guidance to keep project teams from wandering too far off course or getting in over their heads.

Exhibit 4.1 The Define – Design – Build Process

DEFINE	DESIGN	BUILD
•Business Goal & Performance Requirements		
•Conceptual Design	•New Business Process Design	
•Initial Plan & Budget	•System Prototype & Tech Architecture	•Working System
	•Actual Plan & Budget	•Technical Documentation & User Manual
2 Weeks (Or 2 Days)	**1 Month (or 7 Days)**	**2 Months (or 13 Days)**

Define – The Framework for Action

Now let's explore the details of how project teams combine and use these six core techniques in each step of the Define – Design - Build process. By combining selected core techniques they create useful tactics to get work done and achieve the development plan objectives

It is amazing how often the define phase is overlooked or badly performed in the rush to get a project started. Yet this phase forever after either guides or confuses the project team. When performed well, it provides clarity and greatly increases the chances of project success. When performed badly, confusion reigns, and the project has very little chance of success.

The purpose of the activities in the define phase is to align the system development project with the business strategy. In this phase, the business executive who sponsors the system development project clearly spells out the goal or mission of the project by working with the

CIO and the system builder to identify the performance criteria that the system must meet.

Defining the Project Goal

The project goal should be not a technical goal. It should be a business goal - something that provides a significant business benefit or a set of benefits. It should be stated in a format that identifies an action to be taken and states the expected benefit from that action. Some examples are:

> Strengthen and grow the national accounts program by acquiring customers in vertical market segments A, B, and C.

> Reduce the complexity of the steps involved in the warehouse receiving process to make product available for sale immediately after delivery.

The goal answers the question, "Why should we do this project?" It is a qualitative as opposed to a quantitative statement. Everyone affected by a project quickly understands a well-written goal statement. A goal statement should not be longer than a sentence or two. Do not confuse a project goal with a vision statement. A vision statement is a much broader statement about the organization's purpose and aspirations. A goal is one of the things an organization must accomplish in order to bring its vision to life.

Creating the Strategy

Once a project goal has been defined, the next step is to create a strategy to accomplish it. By definition, the strategy uses the means or capabilities available to the business to achieve certain objectives – in this case, the project goal. Businesses often implement strategies by building systems to obtain the new abilities they need. The sponsoring executive works with the CIO and the project's system builder to define the strategy and the high-level or conceptual system design.

To define a project strategy, begin by listing a set of desired performance criteria that the system should meet in order to accomplish its goal. In Chapter 1 we discussed how Robert Kaplan and David Norton in their famous 1992 Harvard Business Review article, "The Balanced Scorecard – Measures That Drive Performance" defined four perspectives that create a comprehensive view of an organization's performance. It's helpful to describe the system's desired performance criteria from these four perspectives as well:

1) Financial Perspective – what financial measures should the system achieve?

2) Customer Perspective – what do external and internal customers want from the system?

3) Business Perspective – what business processes must the company excel at to accomplish the goal?

4) Learning Perspective – how do people continue to learn and continuously improve their ability to accomplish the goal?

Brainstorm a list of performance criteria for each perspective. Then review the lists and select three to six of the most important performance criteria. These are now the measures of success for the project. A successful project builds a system that meets all these criteria.

Next, strive to achieve these criteria in dramatically new ways by asking the question, " What seems impossible now, but if we could make it possible, would dramatically change the way we do business?" Look for ways to use systems that change the business landscape to give your organization a significant competitive advantage by doing something new and different.

The Conceptual System Design

The conceptual system design literally embodies the strategy you will use to create the system. Whenever possible, good conceptual designs build on systems and procedures already in place. The conceptual design is the high-level outline of a system.

Refer to the seven strategic guidelines for designing systems in Chapter 1 on pg....... Generate several different conceptual designs for systems that meet your specified performance criteria. Express the design as a workflow diagram or a process model.

Further define the high level activities in the workflow by specifying the data that goes into and out of each activity. For each activity, estimate the volume and frequency of the data flows and the source and destination of each data flow. In addition, define the types of people (if any) who will perform the work for each activity. How many people are needed? What are the skill levels of the different types of people? Exhibit 4.2 shows how the system process flows for a proposed e-business system.

Next, decide which activities will be automated, manual, and part automated and part manual. As a rule, people like systems that automate the rote, repetitive tasks and empower them to do problem-solving and decision-making tasks more effectively. People are the spark that animates the system, and technology's role is to support that spark.

Evaluate the computer systems infrastructure that already exists in the organization. Look for ways to build on existing systems that work well enough. The most cost-effective new systems are those that adapt existing systems and deliver valuable new capabilities to an organization quickly and with a minimum of expense.

To get started, select the simplest combinations of technology and business processes that meet your specified performance criteria. Balance the need for simplicity with the need to increase the capacity of the system to handle greater volumes of data and the ability to add new functionality as the business grows. Refine and improve the system as you get feedback and ideas from others.

Exhibit 4.2 System Process Flows

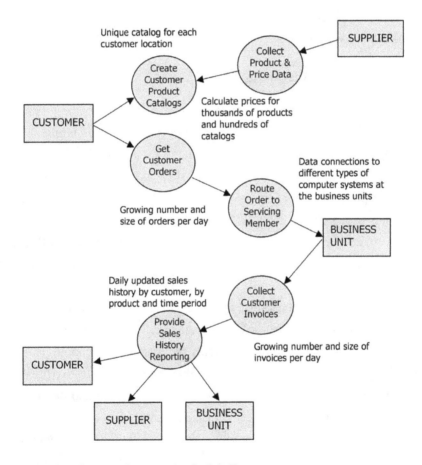

Apply the Seven Strategic Guidelines

Conceptual system designs should respect all of the seven strategic guidelines discussed in Chapter 1. Under some circumstances there may be reasons to violate one or maybe two of these guidelines. The only guideline that can never be violated is the first one – closely align systems development projects with business goals.

If the system devised to accomplish the business goal violates one or two of the guidelines, the executive sponsor and the CIO both must acknowledge these violations and provide justification. A system design that violates only one guideline is acceptable. If it ignores two guidelines, there must be very good reasons for doing so. If it ignores more than two guidelines, the conceptual design is fatally flawed and should be reworked.

Define Project Objectives

When you look at the new workflows and the information system designed to support those workflows, the system resolves into a set of high-level components. Each component should be devoted to the performance of a related set of tasks, such as storing and retrieving data, helping customers find a product, placing an order, or shipping products to customers.

The building of these high-level components becomes the set of necessary and sufficient objectives to create the system you have designed. Projects generally use between three to nine high-level components or objectives, and all other components resolve into sub-components of these high-level components. Strive for no more than three to nine high-level components because most people cannot quickly comprehend or easily remember more than seven (plus or minus two) things at a time. Clarity of system definition and the related objectives is critical to the success of the project.

If the define phase produces a system definition so complex that only a genius can understand it, the definition is useless. Project team members will not be able to use it effectively to guide their work in the next two phases. Without a clear system definition, people on the project team will have different interpretations about what the project is meant to accomplish. People working on different objectives will find it increasingly difficult to coordinate their actions, and the level of tension and argument will rise as the project continues.

The objectives selected should each be achievable in nine months or less. Each objective should provide value in its own right. An objective should not be just an intermediate step that depends on the completion of a subsequent step to be of value. Select objectives that can be achieved quickly because they begin providing value and repaying the cost of the project before it is even finished. Once achieved, an objective becomes a base from which other objectives can be achieved.

Avoid defining objectives that lock the project into a rigid sequence of development activities. The real world rarely goes according to plan, so an agile plan must be flexible in order to adapt as reality unfolds. Begin work on a handful of objectives at the same time (work on objectives in parallel). Design the tasks needed to achieve one objective independent of the tasks needed to achieve other objectives. This provides maximum flexibility. Delays achieving one objective do not affect the completion of other parallel objectives. This way the system builder can shift resources from one objective to another as needed, and the project continues to move forward.

The system conceptual design shown in Exhibit 4.3 has four high level components numbered on the diagram. Each of these components provides value in its own right, and work on each component proceeds independently of the others. These four components become the four objectives for the system developers to achieve in order to create the system shown in this conceptual design.

Work on each of the four objectives or subsystems can proceed in parallel. This way a delay in one or another of the subsystems does not interfere with or slow down work on the other subsystems. Each subsystem can go into production on its own and provide value and as they all come on line, they combine to create the overall system architecture that is needed to achieve the business goal.

Exhibit 4.3 E-Business Systems Infrastructure

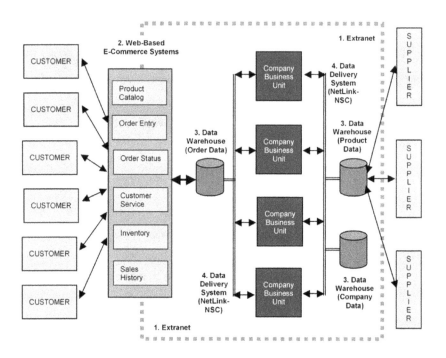

This conceptual design defines four objectives (they are numbered). Each objective can provide value in its own right. They can also be built simultaneously and independently of each other.

The greatest business value lay in the construction of the data warehouse to house the supply chain data and in building the data delivery system called "NetLink-NSC™." Those components working together would best meet the supply chain performance criteria defined by the company. In order to meet financial performance criteria and reduce project risk, it was decided to lease the use of an existing Web-based product catalog and order entry system instead of building one from scratch.

In building the NetLink-NSC™ system people reused parts of an earlier system that provided for electronic receipt and error checking of customer invoices from the business units.

Create Initial Plan and Budget

Once the set of project objectives have been defined, a high-level project plan can be created. Create a section of the overall plan for each objective. In the section of the plan devoted to each objective, list the major tasks necessary to achieve that objective. There will be tasks related to designing and building the deliverables necessary for each objective. Show the dependencies between the tasks and between the objectives. The plan now reflects the strategy being used for building the systems needed to accomplish the business goal. The plan also defines the time boxes for the design and build phase of the project.

Estimate the total project budget by calculating the time and cost needed to achieve each project objective. Each task that is part of the plan for an objective will require some number of people for some period of time. Each task will also require certain technology and perhaps other expenses, such as travel, hotel rooms, and meals. Create a spreadsheet to show the project cost by task for each objective.

After estimating your costs, do a cost-benefit analysis. If it is hard to quantify the different kinds of benefits provided by the system, take this as a warning that the goal of the system has not been well defined or is not very valuable. If the costs of the system outweigh the benefits, find a cheaper and simpler way to accomplish the goal. Avoid the use of expensive technology with more features than are really necessary to get the job done. Exhibit 4.4 shows a summary overview of the work in the define phase.

Outputs of the Define Phase

The agile CIO consistently expects five concrete outputs from the define phase work before moving forward to the design phase. They are:

> *Clear statement of the business goal* to be accomplished.

> *System performance criteria needed to accomplish goal* – these criteria usually fall into four measurement perspectives: 1) financial results; 2) customer expectations; 3) critical business operations; and 4) learning and continuous improvement. These identify and communicate the conditions of success that the system must meet.

> *Conceptual design for a system to accomplish the goal* and meet the performance criteria. The system design is composed of people, process, and technology. The conceptual design is the embodiment of the strategy being used to attain the goal.

> *Definition of the project objectives* that are necessary and sufficient to build the system. Objectives are those items that must be built to create the system outlined in the conceptual design.

> *A cost-benefit and project budget* verifying that the project is worth doing. The senior business executive responsible for accomplishing the business goal that the system will address must confirm that this analysis is valid.

Exhibit 4.4 DEFINE Step

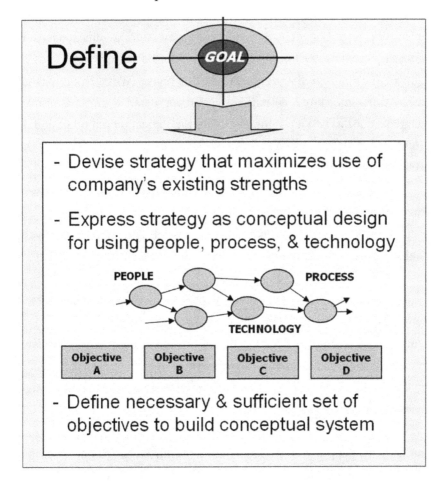

Design – Workflow and Technical System

The purpose of the design phase is to flesh out the conceptual design and create the detailed technical system specifications. The phase begins with the system builder reviewing the project goal, the conceptual system design, and the project objectives with the project work group. The work group is composed of business and technical people who have the necessary mix of business and technical skills and experience needed to do the detailed system design.

It is important for people to understand senior management's intentions and the project's goal. Specific issues relating to the project objectives and budget can be investigated during this phase. If necessary, some adjustments can be made to the project objectives in light of the findings that come out of this phase. Work in the design phase falls into three activities: 1) Create detailed process model diagrams for the new system; 2) Define the logical data model; and 3) Build and test the system prototype i.e., the user interface and the technical architecture.

Divide the total time allotted to the design phase among these three activities. Allocate the necessary time to competently complete each activity avoiding the temptation to spend extra time excessively analyzing and checking and re-checking the results that come out of each activity.

It is important to keep the people involved in these three activities working together. System process models, system data models, and system prototypes are just different aspects of the same system. The designs for these three activities must be created in concert or they will not function properly when assembled. The three design teams must work simultaneously.

Use the joint application design (JAD) technique to integrate the work of people who focus on the three different activities. As the modeling team defines the details of the business process flow, the data modelers can record the data needed by the process. As the process requirements and the data volumes become clear, the technical architecture can be defined and tested to validate how well it supports the process and the data. As the process flow, the data model, and the technical architecture are defined, the prototype team can design the user interface needed to fit the process flow and handle the related data.

The Role of the System Builder

Business and technical people commonly experience a communications gap. The CIO is ultimately responsible for assigning a qualified and competent system builder to lead each development project. The system builder is responsible for creating an inclusive design process that involves both kinds of people and bridging the gap between them. Both business and technical people commonly rush to conclusions about how a process should work or what kind of technology should be used. The system builder must be a person who is able to tolerate not knowing and set an example by reserving judgment and taking the time allocated to select the best of the different design options. When this happens the creative power of the people on the project begins to open up.

The system builder pushes the project teams to keep looking for the simple underlying patterns that define an effective business process. The system builder leads the search for elegantly simple ways to support the process with technology. Remember, more complex systems are harder to build and less likely to succeed.

The Design Process

Spend the first part of the design phase in JAD sessions where business and technical people explore different process designs. People from both disciplines should "think outside of the box" and generate as many ideas as possible. The team then selects the most useful ideas and fits them together into a coherent, detailed map of how work will be organized and flow through the business process.

After sketching out the process work flows, the JAD sessions focus on how technology will be used to support this process. The design team starts by defining how people in the process will interact with the technology supporting the process. Often, designing this user interface takes the form of creating a sequence of screens like a storyboard that people will use in their jobs as they perform their work.

When designing the user interface, look for ways to automate the rote and repetitive work. People don't like to do this kind of work – it is usually boring and computers do these kinds of tasks very well. Look for ways to empower the problem solving and decision-making tasks. Design systems that give people a rewarding work experience.

If the JAD team decides to use a packaged software application, that package should be brought in and installed in a test environment. Script out realistic usage scenarios and load the databases used by the package with a sampling of real data. People who will both use and support the package need to evaluate it by working through the usage scenarios.

The technical people responsible for building the system should sit in on the JAD sessions. As the design unfolds, they should be selecting technology – hardware, operating systems, databases, and other software that will effectively support the system being designed. They should participate and listen to what the business people need to do their jobs. They should not slow down or confuse the design process with excessively technical questions or long dissertations.

During the design phase it may become clear that a given performance criteria cannot be met. It may become clear that the initial conceptual design from the define phase is not quite right and must be modified. Accordingly, certain project objectives might require redefinition. The project goal must remain unchanged but the specific objectives needed to accomplish the goal can be changed as needed. The system builder is the liaison between senior management and the project work group at every step in this redefinition process.

Creation of the Detailed Project Plan and Budget

As the detailed design specifications emerge near the end of the design phase, everyone involved should have a clear idea of their work and the time they need to accomplish it in the subsequent build phase. The system builder then instructs each team to define how they will do their work and how long it will take, challenging them to set ambitious but achievable time frames.

Encourage teams to break their work into discreet tasks that take one week or less because the week is the standard unit of time in business. Teams must strive to accomplish something of measurable value each week to maintain their momentum. A project plan that clearly lays out performance expectations for every person every week is a valuable tactic for coordinating and monitoring the work of building the system. A plan at this level of detail is also the best way to arrive at an accurate and realistic project budget for the build phase.

As the project teams each create their specific task plans to achieve the objectives assigned to them, the system builder combines these plans into the overall project plan. In a process somewhat analogous to the manner in which a general plans a campaign, the system builder plans the sequence of activities that leads to the successful building of the system specified in the design phase.

Divide or segment the overall project plan by objective. Devote a section of the plan to each objective. The system builder determines the best sequence for achieving the project objectives and arranges the project plan to reflect this sequence. Then the task plans created by the project teams assigned to each objective are inserted into the sections of the project plan devoted to their objective.

Look for opportunities to run activities in parallel. Flexible, agile projects accomplish more work simultaneously. When projects run activities sequentially, a delay in one activity causes a ripple effect that delays all the other activities queued up behind it. When activities are run in parallel, a delay in one does not delay the others.

In well-designed project plans, deliverables come together and combine at the end to achieve the objective. Running activities in parallel allows project teams the opportunity to finish one activity and then shift resources over to help out other teams that experience delays. Delays are inevitable on any project. Any plan that fails to account for delays and provide team members the flexibility to effectively respond to them is a plan whose timetable and budget will quickly be thrown into disarray.

The Decision to Proceed, or Not to Proceed

If doubts arise about the viability of the project or if the revised budget has grown too large, reduce the scope of the project or cancel it altogether. At this point only 20% to 40% of the total project cost will have been incurred. The business has yet to commit the major effort on the project. Pay special attention to projects with viability or budget issues whenever they occur.

It is all too common for organizations to run the design phase as a poorly defined research project. Teams spend a great deal of time in detailed analysis of what already exists but produce only sketchy designs for the specifics of the new system. Debates break out on many aspects of the design of the new system, but no one can agree on clear answers and critical decisions are not made or are pushed into the build phase.

Use the design phase as an opportunity to reduce the risk on a project before committing large amounts of time and money. The more detailed the design specifications the better the chances for building the system on time and on budget. The broader the understanding of and support for the system among both the business and the technical people, the greater the likelihood that the system will be used effectively and produce the desired business results. Exhibit 4.5 illustrates the activities in the design phase.

Design Phase Deliverables

The agile CIO expects four detailed deliverables from design phase work before approving a project for the build phase.

Detailed design of the new business process flows supported by the system. Make sure there is agreement among the people who will have to work with the system that it will meet the performance criteria expected of it. The specifications for the business process are created using the process mapping technique and captured in documents such as process flow diagrams and process logic descriptions for each step in the process.

System data model that accommodates the data identified by the process map. The data model should be created using an entity-relationship diagram (ERD) that other people on the project can understand. The model should also record the volume of data that will be handled and the frequency with which different types of data will be accessed.

System prototype that specifies both the technical architecture and the user interface. There should be a development environment in operation where all the components of the technical architecture are installed and working together. This technical architecture must be capable of handling the anticipated data volumes and user demands. Define the user interface needed to support the process logic in the relevant steps of the process flow. There must be a complete set of screen layouts, report formats, and specifications for all aspects of the user interface.

Detailed project plan and budget that accurately reflects the time, cost, and resources needed to build the system. No plan can predict the future or anticipate all obstacles, and no budget can accurately estimate every cost. However, plans and budgets built up from the detail task level and structured to provide as much flexibility as possible are essential to guiding the project to a successful conclusion. 30-day budgets can be very accurate.

Exhibit 4.5 DESIGN Phase

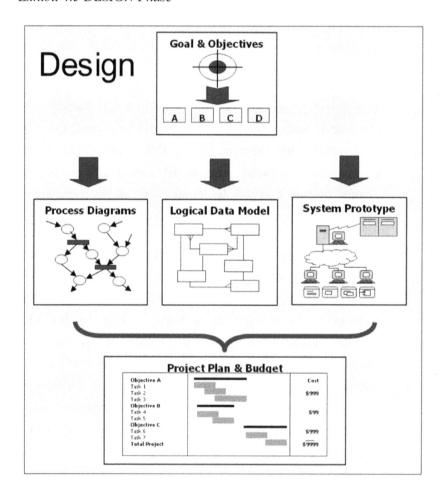

Build – System Construction and Roll Out

The project effort really ramps up in the build phase. The full compliment of people is brought on to fill out the project teams. Consequently, the weekly cost or "burn rate" on the project rises significantly in the build phase. Unlike the previous two phases, the cost of false starts and wrong turns now adds up very quickly.

This is where your system builder vigorously exercises project leadership skills. Activity must be tightly focused on the completion of those defined tasks necessary to achieve the project objectives. In this phase, good design and planning pay off handsomely.

The System Blueprints

The initial work in this phase creates the system object model from the combination of specifications from the data model and the system prototype. This activity is often started in the design phase as part of the detail design and budgeting process. By completing the work at the appropriate level of detail, the project teams produce very exact blueprints of what they will build. This strengthens the teams' understanding of and confidence in their ability to complete the work according to plan.

System blueprints take the form of the screen layouts, database design, system object model, and detailed technical architecture diagrams. These documents guide and structure the work that creates the actual system. The system builder and the team leaders track their progress every week using these documents to discuss relevant details.

Teams create and test system database and software in the system development environment. The development environment created in the design phase supports the prototyping of the technical architecture and the user interface with the actual hardware, operating systems, and database packages used to build the system. Preprogrammed application software packages used for parts or all of the system also are installed and tested in the development environment.

Once programming begins, record progress at the object level using the object chart as the reporting tool. Circle an object as work begins. Everyone can see how long the work should take. Color in objects when work has been completed. People can see software development progress at a glance by looking at the object model. When problems develop the system builder and team leaders can use the object model to quickly see what issues affect each object. They can then focus on specific solutions for well-defined problems.

If software development projects are not tracked at this level of detail, people resort to the infamous "percentage complete" method. Under this method, large multi-week tasks quickly become "70% complete" (whatever that means). Then the last 30% takes four times as long to finish as the first 70%, and nobody can figure out why.

The Project Office

The system builder effectively coordinates and focuses activities on a fast paced project through the project office. The CIO uses the project office to accurately manage a portfolio of IT development projects. The project office employs a skilled staff dedicated solely to working with the system builder and the team leaders to update the project plan and budget as work progresses.

The system builder is analogous to the general manager of a business unit, and the project office is like the accounting department. The general manager does not have time to keep the business unit's books nor is that the general manager's job. But if no one keeps the books, the general manager looses touch with where the business really stands and this inevitably leads to bad decisions.

There is a pervasive tendency for people to hide bad news such as delays and cost over-runs. Trouble results unless leadership takes active steps to counter this tendency. People should not be penalized for reporting bad news. On the contrary, leaders who give their people permission and encouragement to report delays and potential cost over-runs as soon as they perceive them improve the entire project's chances of success because everyone has more time to react.

Early reporting gives everyone more time to respond and respond effectively. The project office staff exists to help people keep track of actual project progress and make good decisions with the information the project office provides. Indeed, one of the best ways to get into trouble is to hide bad news because when the truth finally does come out, there is usually very little (if any) time to respond effectively to the situation.

System Test and Rollout

As major system components or subsystems are delivered, they are beta tested with a pilot group of business people involved since the design phase of the project. In this way they already understand and except the need for and benefits of the new system making them effective beta test personnel.

Expect to make adjustments to the system architecture and to the user interface during the beta test. People who operate the system architecture will need to tweak different operating parameters to get the best response time and stability from the system. People who designed the user interface will need to sit down with the beta test group of business users and listen to their ideas for improvements to certain screens.

Business people in the pilot group smooth off the rough edges as they test the system and make suggestions for adjustments. In this process, advocates for the system emerge from among the beta test group. They will feel a personal connection to the success of the system because the system will take on a look and feel influenced by their suggestions. These people will sell the benefits of the system to the rest of the company and often become the ones to train their co-workers to use the new system. Exhibit 4.6 shows the operation of the build phase.

Lead By Staying Involved

The CIO relies on a mixture of information from the updated project plans, budgets, personal visits, and investigations into projects that attract attention. Effective CIOs cannot spend undue time in their office reading e-mails and writing reports. Effective CIOs hold regular meetings with all their system builders to review progress on projects, and as problems arise, the CIO continuously assesses when to get personally involved and when to delegate to others.

Inevitably, obstacles arise and delays happen. The agile CIO demands flexibility in the project plans and uses people that can be shifted from one project objective to another and in this way retains more options. Systems that use simple combinations of technology and business process to achieve multiple objectives are more likely to be built on time and on budget. With systems like this, CIOs can quickly shift resources from one project to another because the same skill sets and technologies are being used to achieve different objectives.

Build Phase Deliverables

Agile CIOs expect three critical deliverables from the build phase work.

> *Working system that matches the design specifications and meets the performance criteria.* Schedule the building of the system so that the process delivers something of value to the business every 30 – 90 days. This means that certain pieces of the system must be finished and put into use before the entire system is completed.

Complete and updated set of technical design documents; design documentation is analogous to the wiring diagrams and structural plans of a building. This documentation enables the IT organization to build enhancements and make repairs to the system in the future. The documentation should include at least the object model, the data model, an organized library of program source code, and diagrams and descriptions of the overall process flow of the system.

Complete set of user and operating instructions; people who operate and maintain a system are different from the people who build systems. The people who operate a system need to know how bring the system up, bring it down, and carry out performance tuning, trouble shooting, and operating maintenance. Assign the people responsible for operating a new system to work with the development team during system rollout to define the needed operating and maintenance documentation. ∞

Exhibit 4.6 BUILD Phase

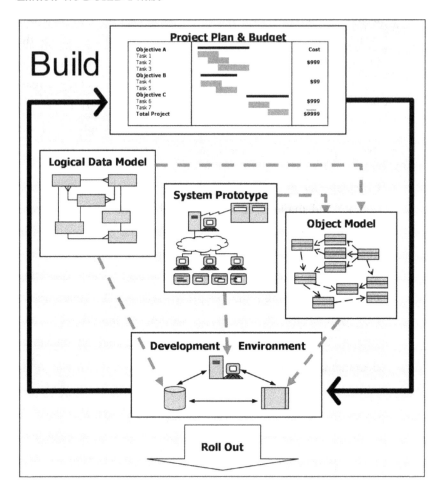

Notes and Ideas for Action:

Notes and Ideas for Action:

Chapter 5.

Encounter with Complexity

I'll use four real projects from my own experience to examine what works and what doesn't work when it comes to developing new systems using the principles discussed in this book. All of these projects were high visibility, multi-million dollar system development projects. I was the overall project leader or system builder on three of them. On the fourth I was one of four team leaders – there was no overall system builder. These four projects span a fifteen year period; two were major successes, one was a catastrophic failure, and one, though not a complete failure, was not a ringing success either.

These projects used a range of technologies - IBM mainframes with COBOL and DB2, Sun servers running Java and Sybase, and Windows servers with SQL Server databases accessed through PCs and Web-based thin clients. I presently use these agile principles illustrated here to develop cloud-based apps using Ruby-on-Rails and MySQL accessed by mobile devices. Although the technology and the business goals were different for each project, I began to see consistent reasons for project successes and failures. A timeline analysis of these four projects demonstrates the importance of applying the agile principles discussed in this book. Agile project timelines are practical and realistic, and their use significantly reduces the risk of catastrophic failures. I learned these lessons the hard way. But what other way is there to learn such lessons?

Case Studies: Two Wins, A Lose and a Draw

I learned that the seven strategic system guidelines and the six principles for running projects really work and that there are consequences when they are ignored. I also saw that the core techniques (the skills of the game) were applicable each time regardless of the technology being used. These guidelines, principles, and core techniques represent a body of knowledge that must be understood and applied to successfully create a new system.

Finally, I saw that there is a basic, underlying sequence to the process of building computer systems. That sequence is Define-Design-Build. Depending on the system development methodology or the consulting company facilitating development of the new system, there could officially be a much more complicated process in place but the added complexity leads to trouble. Simplicity is the key to success in multidisciplinary projects prone to layers of different interpretations for both business and technological participants.

Define-Design-Build remedies the tendency to make projects more complex. In a more complicated development process the Define phase can be divided into two or more steps with important sounding names such as "Preliminary Needs Analysis" or "System Concept Justification". The Design phase may be fractured into three or four steps with more fancy titles and the Build phase can be broken into a further number of steps.

This added complexity neither increases peoples' chances of success nor changes the basic sequence of events that have to occur. First, one must still define what is to be done. Next, one must still design how it will be done. And lastly, one must still build it.

The following charts in Exhibits 5.1 through 5.4 are maps of the four projects. They show how each project unfolded over time. Study the sequence of activities and read the notes that explain these activities for an overall appreciation of each project. Underneath every chart is a brief description of what happened. Look for the ways that successful projects consistently applied the principles, and try to pinpoint where the failed and partially successful projects lost focus.

Takeaway Lessons

What can be learned here? To begin with, every project needs a qualified, full time project leader or system builder who has full responsibility and day-to-day authority for running the entire project. Working with the senior businessperson sponsoring the project, the system builder identifies a specific business opportunity and defines the system performance criteria needed to exploit that opportunity.

Projects should focus on developing new system capabilities not already available in existing systems. For the best results, combine new technology with existing systems to create new systems. Avoid recreating functions that already exist in older systems that work well enough. You run up too many costs and deliver too little value when you rip out existing systems and replace them with new technology that does essentially the same things.

By building upon existing systems, a much simpler set of new technology can often be used. PC workstations can be used to run terminal emulation software giving people access existing mainframe systems. New applications can be Web or server based. The whole mix of new and old applications can be integrated under a single graphical user interface by giving each application an icon that users click on to switch from one application to another. This architecture can be easily extended via application program interfaces (APIs) to run as apps on mobile devices.

Employ the time-boxes suggested in the Define-Design-Build process and move the project along at a fast clip. It is very important to set and maintain a brisk pace on a project to prevent it from degenerating into a sluggish and indecisive voyage to nowhere. Use the overall time-boxes for each phase and then subdivide these boxes into smaller boxes for each of the major activities defined in a phase. Further subdivide those activity time-boxes into task level time-boxes. The trick is to define time-boxes that are both aggressive and realistic.

Both of the projects that succeeded shared a very effective approach. Simply stated, this approach first focuses the development effort to create a breakthrough deliverable – a deliverable that proves the system and wins over lots of supporters. After achieving the breakthrough deliverable, make every effort to exploit it quickly by developing more system enhancements and new subsystems to address further opportunities opened up by the breakthrough.

These case studies also show projects where work runs in parallel on several subsystems is better than stringing out the work and developing each subsystem in a long sequence. When you design each subsystem so that it can go into production on its own and provide value all by itself then you know at least some of the projects will finish on time. As other subsystems that might have been delayed are completed and go into production, they connect with and build upon what is already in place. This is both the fastest and least risky way to get things done.

The slow sequential approach seems less risky at first, but you soon learn it is not.

Exhibit 5.1 Enterprise Sales Support System – A Win

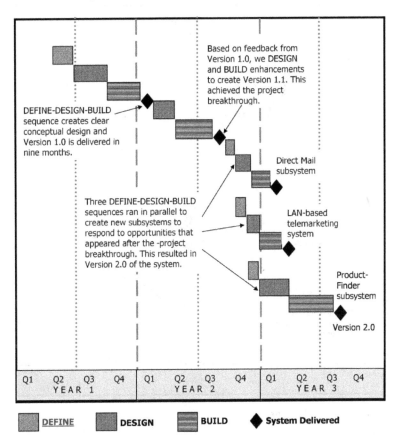

This development sequence narrowed scope and focused resources up front to create version one of the system and achieve the project breakthrough point. Once the breakthrough had been achieved, multiple DEFINE-DESIGN-BUILD sequences were launched in parallel to exploit the opportunities that opened up.

I followed all the strategic design guidelines. The tactical principles for running projects were followed although there was no staff devoted exclusively to the project office function. The team leaders and I did the project office work and at times we did not keep plans and budgets up to date. If the project had been any larger, the lack of dedicated project office staff would have hurt us.

Exhibit 5.2 Web-Enables Supply Chain – A Win

DEFINE created a conceptual system design to accomplish e-business goal.

Strategic planning exercise

Beta test data warehouse & sales history reporting

Ver 1.0 NetLink

DEFINE phase identified four system components and DESIGN-BUILD sequences ran in parallel to produce version 1.0 of these components. Project breakthrough was achieved.

Ver 1.0 Data Warehouse

New web site

Tech Infrastructure

Version 1.0 of E-Business Systems

DESIGN-BUILD creates version 1.1 enhancements to two system components

NetLink Enhancements

Data Warehouse Enhancements

Data Warehouse Enhancements

Web Site Enhancements

DEFINE-DESIGN-BUILD creates version 2.0 enhancements to exploit further business opportunities.

NetLink Enhancements

Q3	Q4	Q1	Q2	Q3	Q4	Q1	Q2	Q3	Q4	Q1	Q2
				YEAR 1				YEAR 2			

DEFINE   **DESIGN**   BUILD   ◆ **System Delivered**

The development sequence was focused and tightly time-boxed. Work ran in parallel during the DESIGN-BUILD phases requiring good planning and coordination. Version 1.0 of systems infrastructure created in nine months. Positive reception and feedback from version 1.0, let to enhancements for version 1.1. New business opportunity led to next round of enhancements that created version 2.0 of the e-business systems infrastructure.

I followed all of the seven strategic design guidelines and respected the six tactical principles for running projects. This project was a clear demonstration of how to quickly and cost effectively design and build a suite of new systems that then provide significant competitive advantage.

Exhibit 5.3 New Technology for Sales Project – A Lose

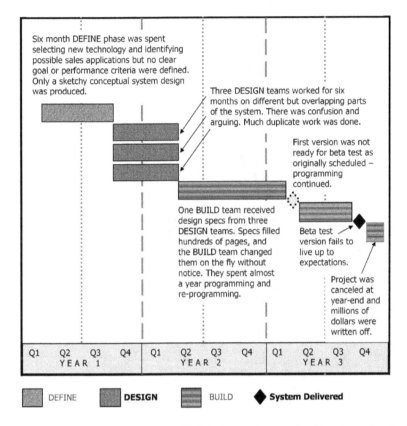

Six month DEFINE phase was spent selecting new technology and identifying possible sales applications but no clear goal or performance criteria were defined. Only a sketchy conceptual system design was produced.

Three DESIGN teams worked for six months on different but overlapping parts of the system. There was confusion and arguing. Much duplicate work was done.

First version was not ready for beta test as originally scheduled – programming continued.

One BUILD team received design specs from three DESIGN teams. Specs filled hundreds of pages, and the BUILD team changed them on the fly without notice. They spent almost a year programming and re-programming.

Beta test version fails to live up to expectations.

Project was canceled at year-end and millions of dollars were written off.

| Q1 | Q2 | Q3 | Q4 | Q1 | Q2 | Q3 | Q4 | Q1 | Q2 | Q3 | Q4 |
| YEAR 1 | | | | YEAR 2 | | | | YEAR 3 | | | |

☐ DEFINE   ▨ **DESIGN**   ▤ BUILD   ◆ **System Delivered**

On this project there was a long DEFINE phase that resulted in a broad project scope. There was no clear focus of effort. Resources were then spread across several different DESIGN teams who developed complex designs. Design specifications were handed off to a BUILD team that was overwhelmed by the amount of work required. Momentum was lost and a breakdown occurred in the BUILD phase. Programmers worked long and hard but the project never recovered.

I was one of four team leaders. There was no overall project manager or system builder to answer questions or resolve disputes. The strategic design guidelines were completely ignored – some deliberately and some out of carelessness. Most of the tactical principles for running projects were violated. Project teams did have 2-7 people and we did have freedom to figure out how to do our work, but we still did not know exactly what we were supposed to do. So everything took forever.

Exhibit 5. Next Gen Financial Services System – A Draw

Partnership formed with high-tech company to provide advanced information technology. There was great enthusiasm and a rush to get started.

Performance of first beta test version was unacceptable – response time was very slow.

Project team of people from company and high-tech partner designed and built first version of system.

Beta test system worked but did not generate much enthusiasm. There was no project breakthrough.

Project was reorganized and re-energized. The project goal and system performance criteria were clarified. New project leader was put in charge.

The system and related business assets were sold for several million dollars to recoup some of the project expenses.

| Q1 | Q2 | Q3 | Q4 | Q1 | Q2 | Q3 | Q4 | Q1 | Q2 | Q3 | Q4 |
| | YEAR 1 | | | | YEAR 2 | | | | YEAR 3 | | |

DEFINE   **DESIGN**   **BUILD**   ◆ **System Delivered**

The project got off to an adequate start, but then faltered because the technology did not perform up to expectations and the business logic was not accurately captured during the DESIGN phase. The project was reorganized and re-energized but no fundamental changes were made in technology or project scope. The renewed effort produced some better results but not enough to gain acceptance of the system from target customers.

I was the new project leader brought in when project was reorganized. I followed the tactical principles for running projects and applied them vigorously. The project was closely aligned with a business goal and there was some flexibility in both the project plan and the project staff. However, the other five strategic guidelines were not followed. I learned what many have learned before – great tactics cannot make up for flawed strategy.

Executive Checklist for Monitoring Development Projects

Executives who sponsor system development projects need a way to assess them as they move through the Define, Design, and Build sequence. These questions and the answers provided can be used to assess any IT development project, and they will reveal quite clearly whether things are going well.

The questions listed here will enable you to assess development projects from three perspectives that cover all the important aspects of system development. Those three perspectives are: 1) Goodness of system design; 2) Progress made developing the system; and 3) Competence and confidence of people on the project.

Goodness of System Design

In the first two to six weeks of the project—the Define phase—ask yourself and the system builder in charge of the project these questions:

> 1. What is the business goal of the project? In two sentences or less, state the action the company is going to take and the desired result of that action. This is the goal. It is the target, the destination the project is supposed to reach. Figure out what it is, or stop the project.

> 2. Which performance criteria is the system supposed to meet? State requirements that the system will meet in these areas: a) Business operations; b) Customer expectations; c) Financial performance; and d) Company learning and improvement. These are the specific measures that will determine whether the

system will be a success. Make sure that you and the people designing and building the system know what they are.

3. Do you believe that a system that meets the preceding performance requirements will accomplish the business goal you are striving for? If you have a feeling that important performance requirements have been left out, add them before the project gets any further along, but make sure that you add only requirements that are strictly necessary to accomplish the business goal. Requirements that are too broad will result in increased system complexity and less chance that the system can be built successfully.

4. Which existing computer systems in your company does the new system design leverage? The new system should leverage the strengths of systems and procedures already in place. That way it can focus on delivering new capabilities instead of just replacing something that already exists. If you decide to replace everything and build from a clean slate, you had better be prepared for the considerable extra time and expense involved and be sure that it's worth it.

5. Does the overall design for the new system break down into a set of self-contained subsystems that can each operate on its own and provide value? Large computer systems are really made up of a bunch of smaller subsystems. Your company should be able to build each subsystem independently of the others. That way, if one subsystem runs into problems, work on the others can still proceed. As subsystems are completed, they should be put into production as soon as possible to begin paying back the expense of building them. If all subsystems must be complete before any can be put to use, that's a very risky, all-or-nothing system design. Change it.

6. How accurate is the cost-benefit analysis for the new system? Have the business benefits been overstated? Would the project still be worth doing if the business benefits were only half of those predicted? Cost-benefit calculations usually understate costs and overstate benefits. You are the one who is best able to judge the validity of the calculations. Do you believe they are accurate? The bigger and riskier the project, the greater the benefits must be to justify the risks and expense. Don't spend more on a system than it's worth.

7. How has the system builder demonstrated that his or her system design and project leadership skills are appropriate to the demands of the project? If you don't have a qualified system builder in charge, the project will fail from lack of direction. Management by committee won't work. If this person lacks the necessary design and leadership skills, he or she must be replaced, no matter what other skills the person may possess.

8. Which of the strategic guidelines have been followed, and which have not? If you follow all seven of the strategic guidelines are followed (see Appendix B), the design of the system is very good. It's acceptable if one of the guidelines—except the first one—isn't followed. If two aren't followed, there had better be very good reasons. In that case, determine which extra precautions will be taken to compensate for the increased risk. If more than two of the guidelines aren't followed, the design is fatally flawed. The system can't be built on time or on budget, if it can be built at all.

Progress Made Developing the System

As the project moves through the design and build phases, ask yourself, the system builder, and the project teams these questions:

1. Are the project plan and budget in place? Do people pay attention to the plan? Is there a project office group that provides regular and accurate updates to the plan and the budget? Multimillion-dollar system development projects involve a lot of people and stretch across some period of time. The project plan is the central coordinating instrument that tells every person exactly what he or she is supposed to be doing at any given time. If the plan isn't kept current, the people on the project have no way to coordinate their work effectively. The system builder will lose track of the details. Delays, cost overruns, and confusion will result. People won't know how much has been spent to date or how much more is required to finish. When this happens, the project goes into a death spiral.

2. Are the subsystem teams organizing their work into clearly defined design and build phases? Are these phases getting done on time and on budget? The project team working on each subsystem should spend one to three months creating a detailed design and system prototype (Design phase). The detailed design should then be turned into a working system within two to six months (Build phase). If things take longer than this, the project is moving too slowly and it will lose momentum and drift. It's the system builder's responsibility to keep things organized and moving. Make sure this person is capable.

3. What's the situation this week? Spot-check the project plan and budget from time to time. Have the system builder review the current project plan with you, show you the money spent to

date on each subsystem, and the estimate for remaining time and budget to complete each subsystem. Do you believe what you hear? Can the system builder explain the situation clearly, without tech talk? How does the most recent estimate of time and budget compare to original estimates? Is it still worth the cost to complete the project?

Competence and Confidence of the Project Team

Ask these questions of yourself, the system builder, and the project teams:

1. What are the design specifications? As each project team completes its Design phase, ask them to show you the design specifications, the process flow diagrams, the logical data model for their subsystem, the user interface, the technical architecture diagrams, and the system prototype. Can they tell you how this system will deliver the business benefits in the cost-benefit analysis? Do the design specifications make any sense? Do the people on the team know what they're talking about?

2. Are the project team members as confident as the project team leaders? Are the team leaders as confident as the system builder? If people believe they have the right skills and a good system design, they will be confident in their ability to build the system. If people at every level don't share and reflect this confidence, there's a problem somewhere. If people are trying to transfer onto the project, that demonstrates confidence. If people are transferring off the project or leaving the company, that indicates lack of confidence. Expect the project to fail. ∞

Notes and Ideas for Action:

About the Author

MICHAEL HUGOS is an author, speaker, award-winning CIO and principal at Center for Systems Innovation [c4si]. He works with clients to find elegant solutions to complex problems and mentors development teams in agile techniques. His focus is in supply chains, business intelligence, and new business ventures. Earlier he spent six years as CIO of a national distribution organization where he developed a suite of supply chain and e-business systems that transformed the company's operations and revenue model. For this work he won the CIO 100 Award for resourcefulness, the InformationWeek 500 Award for innovation, and the Computerworld Premier 100 Award for career achievement..

Michael earned his MBA from Northwestern University's Kellogg School of Management. He regularly contributes to industry publications and websites, and is the author of several other books, including the popular Essentials of Supply Chain Management, 3rd Edition and his book, Business in the Cloud: What Every Business Needs to Know about Cloud Computing. He can be reached via his website - www.MichaelHugos.com
email him at mhugos@yahoo.com

Other Books by Michael Hugos

Enterprise Games: Using Game Mechanics to Build a Better Business, Center for Systems Innovation [c4si], 2013

Business in the Cloud: What Every Business Needs to Know About Cloud Computing, Wiley, 2011

Essentials of Supply Chain Management, 3rd Edition, Wiley, 2011

CIO Best Practices: Enabling Strategic Value with Information Technology, Wiley, 2010

Business Agility: Sustainable Prosperity in a Relentlessly Competitive World, Wiley, 2009

Building the Real Time Enterprise: An Executive Briefing, Wiley, 2005

All are available as Kindle books or printed books on Amazon.com

Notes and Ideas for Action:

Notes and Ideas for Action:

www.ingramcontent.com/pod-product-compliance
Lightning Source LLC
Chambersburg PA
CBHW071005050326
40689CB00014B/3494